LIFT
Launch
Lead

THE ULTIMATE FAITH-BASED
ENTREPRENEUR'S GUIDE

LIFT
Launch
Lead

THE ULTIMATE FAITH-BASED
ENTREPRENEUR'S GUIDE

WILLIAMS | HICKS IZZARD | JONES

LIFT Launch Lead: The Ultimate Faith-Based Entrepreneur's Guide

Published by LIFT Enterprises

Unless otherwise indicated, scripture quotations are from the Holy Bible, King James Version. All rights reserved.

Scriptures marked NIV are taken from the New International Version®. Copyright © 1973, 1978, 1984, 2011 by Biblica, Inc.™ All Rights Reserved.

ISBN for Paperback: 978-1-7335065-2-6
ISBN for E-Book: 978-1-7335065-3-3

Printed in the United States of America

Contents

Preface
By Kim Jones

LIFT Launch Lead: The Ultimate Faith-Based Entrepreneur's Guide is an extraordinary book about phenomenal women who have taken astonishing leaps of faith in their lives and businesses. It covers their initial steps, their investments and the sacrifices of their time and talent. The women tell of the strategies and tools that have equipped them to move steadfastly from devastating situations towards launching new ventures, building and taking risks. Boldly, the authors show how they are achieving good success by faith.

This book is written because there is a pressing need to break out of the box and to hear from successful women to LIFT Launch and Lead. It is intended to inspire women who are educated, credentialed, skilled and accomplished to go to the next level. We hope to assist goal-oriented women to clearly define and express the vision that God gave them. Whether they are ready to establish their own business, ministry or movement, this book will guide women to achieve greater success.

Many entrepreneurs have made poor choices; they have experienced misfortune and need coaching and mentoring to assist in turning their business and life around. As you read each compelling story, you will quickly discover this is not a book about tips and tricks to fit a specific model of success. Instead, these awesome women have confidently written about *LIFTing* you to believing that if they can succeed you can too. The authors are about *Launching* you into your God-given vision and *Leading* you to live victoriously on your terms as a result of your blood, sweat, and tears.

Maybe you stopped believing, or maybe you have given up, and this book is just the motivation you need to start again. These stories are stories of faith and encouragement of women just like you to *LIFT Launch Lead* you to your next level. We encourage you to trust the process. We know that sometimes there will be uncertainties, but ultimately, we must do whatever is required by any means necessary! My one advice to you on this journey is to keep going towards the mark of the high calling and *TRUST GOD!*

Introduction

By Dr. Ranelli Williams

Many women remain stuck in a dead-end career or in a business that is stagnant because they refuse to untangle themselves from the chains of comfort and break free into adventurous action. The word **LIFT** means to raise to a higher position or level OR pick up and move to a different position. If you are going to LIFT, my sisters, you are going to have to be courageous. You are going to have to step out and make some bold changes. Then and only then will you pivot forward to your next. If you are ready for more, stay with me...

The word **launch** means to start or set an activity or enterprise in motion by pushing it forward. Did you hear that sisters? Your business, your mission, or your purpose will not launch in your mind. You must push it forward. You have to get it out of your heads and hearts. The Bible clearly states in Habakkuk 2 to "Write the vision and make it plain." Therefore, your first call to action is to write out the plans God has placed in your hearts. If you are going to launch something effective and powerful, ladies, you must write it down first. The second thing you need to do is to create a plan of action, and once your plan is in place, you must execute it. Implementing a strategy is synonymous with pushing it forward, so I urge you to get moving.

Furthermore, to **lead** means to be a route or means of access to a particular place or in a particular direction. I just love this definition. Sisters, who are you leading and where are you leading them to? That's a huge responsibility you cannot take lightly. As I think about my own purpose to provide access to couples who are looking to be legends and give their children an advantage by leaving them a legacy of faith, of business ownership, of money mastery, and of generational wealth-building, I realize I cannot do this passively. If I choose to be passive or unsure, then people won't follow and those who decide to follow will either be confused or not be compelled to move expeditiously. I must lead with passion and conviction in order to be effective. You also must lead with confidence to be impactful.

In this book, our goal is to give you a framework to LIFT, Launch, and Lead with excellence in the area(s) you were called to serve. The 17 co-authors who shared their gifts and stories all provide a different perspective of how they took challenging situations in their lives and rose to victory. Recognizing that each of us has a unique story that has brought us to where we are today, these ladies have bravely stepped out to share their journeys because as Cheryl Wood said, "Your message is about you, but it is not for you." These co-authors recognize that by sharing their journey, you might be impacted to LIFT, Launch, and Lead.

Prayerfully their stories will inspire and heal you. We hope reading this book will cause you to be a bold believer as you claim God's plan for your life. God said in His word, "I know the plans I have for you; plans to prosper you and not to harm you" (Jeremiah 29:11 NIV). Therefore, you need to understand that no matter what you have been through in life, you need to muster up the courage and the faith to use it to your advantage. You need to use it as fuel to LIFT, Launch, and Lead into something great.

Your opportunities are endless. However, you must believe that your struggles can be used to activate your purpose and propel you to serve others in a powerful way. Are you ready for an adventure? Let's go!

One Must Leap to Fly

By Donna Heath-Gonzalez

As a little girl growing up on the beautiful island of Jamaica, my parents struggled to provide the necessities of life for us, but they still did—gracefully. The reality I knew did not correlate to the life that I dreamed of living. What I aspired for was the freedom to be myself, travel the world, dress how I wanted and pursue my dreams. The life paths I envisioned that met these criteria were that of a teacher, an air hostess (now known as a flight attendant) or an entrepreneur. Life gives us all chances, slivers of opportunity to become who want to be and who God meant for us to be. For some like me, the way to our purpose may be littered with more obstacles, but ultimately the previous statement holds true. It is our ability to recognize these moments and take action that determines our lot in life.

At the risk of sounding cliché, I'd liken it to a young bird perched at the edge of the branch peering out into the unknown. In theory, it knows there is a possibility that if it leaps it may fly for it has seen other birds do the like. On the flip side, it knows what's at stake if it is not successful. In this space of deliberation, planning, and uncertainty, one thing is for sure; to even have a chance at flying it must first leap. In the scripture it says, faith without works is dead.

For me, this truth has been the most pivotal element in my journey.

I held on to my dreams, persevering through many challenges on my journey to be the person I imagined as a child. At the age of 29, I was the first of my siblings to attend college, a great achievement for my family. It was a very exciting time for me being a mother, a wife and a college student all at the same time. First, I attended a community college where I received an associate degree in Accounting. Upon graduation, I went on to receive my bachelor's degree in Accounting. What a milestone and blessing my educational achievements have been for my family! During and after my collegiate years, I had the opportunity to work in various corporate settings which helped prepare me for entrepreneurship. While on my career path, I found that being an employee would be a short chapter of my journey. My true passion and destiny lied in being a business owner.

In the mid-2000's, I had a great job in the finance department of a major company with the opportunity for growth. After my first year, I embraced that opportunity and accepted the offer for a higher position. Driven to keep growing, I decided to pursue a master's degree which caused my daily life to become difficult – rapidly. Juggling work, school, kids, family, and home while commuting one hour and a half each way to a different state was no small task.

During my commute which started at about 5 a.m., I would do a lot of thinking about my life, future and career. That was my time to have my conversation with God, to thank Him for who He has been in my life, for what He has done, and for how He has kept me thus far. It was also during that time I realized I needed to start researching my entrepreneurship options because doing that long trek to and from work every day was not going to cut it. I really sought God's guidance in this decision-making process because it was a big leap of faith into the unknown, which had me focused on the scripture in Habakkuk 2:2-3 which says, "And the Lord answered me, and said, Write the vision, and make it plain upon tablets, that he may run who reads it. For the vision is yet for an appointed time, but at the end it shall speak, and not lie: though it tarry, wait for it; because it will surely come, it will not tarry." So yes, He did answer me, and yes, He made a way for me to proceed on my entrepreneurship journey.

My next move was to decide which industry best complimented my passion, knowledge, and experience while being profitable. One factor I considered heavily was the risk of starting a business, which was multiplied due to the turbulent state of the economy at the time. I concluded that the most logical business would supply a need, regardless of the state of the economy. At first, my choice was a restaurant serving Caribbean food since I enjoyed cooking, especially that style of cuisine. I thought a restaurant would be an easy transition for me because of my knowledge of the various dishes and my experience cooking for large groups of people. However, after considering the population and demand in my area, I decided against it.

The beauty industry was different because no matter what, health and beauty items are needed for our daily hygiene regimens. I had retail experience but not in the hair care or beauty supply industry. My baseline knowledge in comparison to the restaurant was limited because the only products I knew about were the ones I used. So, I knew this choice would require significant research to gain product knowledge. As I started researching hair and hair product manufacturers, I became fascinated by the options we have to enhance our beauty and developed a passion for it. Throughout the research phase, I was still working, attending graduate school and commuting.

One morning while driving to work, I asked God which of these two options was His will and purpose for my life. He answered me when He reminded me that my life, journey and experiences can be used as testimonies for other women to know that He is a protector, provider, deliverer and a way maker. With that confirmation, I made my decision that my entrepreneurship calling is in the Beauty Supply Industry and thus Big Apple Beauty Supply, Inc. was born.

In early fall of 2007, I contacted the local Small Business Development Center, SCORE Association, Chamber of Commerce and colleges that offered workshops for starting and registering a business in my state. My next move was filing the necessary state registration and establishing accounts with distributors and manufacturers. To gain an understanding of this industry, I decided to test the market before resigning from my job. An easy, low-cost option without excessive overhead was to rent a booth at the local flea market in my area on the weekends. This would allow me to begin marketing my business and brand, build a customer base and determine the products that best fit the needs of the customers in my area. This move was what I called "my on the job training," because as I said before, I had no prior experience in the beauty industry.

As the weeks went by, my motivation and passion for this venture increased and I knew for sure that this was what I wanted to do, and where I belonged. However, due to several reasons, I was having a tough time committing to full-time entrepreneurship. For one, I was thankful for the great income and success at my job, even though the long commute that included hours of traffic was my biggest challenge. I believed that when we pray for God to deliver us from something or to provide us with another option, we must be ready to make the move at any time because if it is His will, He will do it in His timing.

Reflecting on my journey, I believe my decision was finally made when I experienced a terrible fall down a flight of steps, resulting in torn ligaments in my right knee, broken toes, and a sprained ankle. This incident kept me from driving and working for six months and required me to use a walker then a cane to move about. This setback was deeply saddening as I was in the throes of my master's degree coursework, my job and my burgeoning entrepreneurship journey. After two grim weeks post-accident amidst my tears and sorrow, I finally accepted my state of brokenness, setbacks, and pain.

It was difficult seeing myself in that condition, so I prayed and fasted relentlessly. I was looking for answers from God, wondering how this could happen at a time of such positivity and potential. God's answer was profound! He reminded me that He *already* provided me the opportunity to move forward with the business venture. His opportunity, if I accepted it, would deliver me from the long interstate work and pave a path into an industry where I had no prior experience. This answer was my confirmation that "He is a provider, deliver and a way maker."

With this resolve, I spent my recovery time aggressively research-ing the hair and beauty industry, upcoming tradeshow dates, commercial leases, my future store location, my state requirements for doing business, market analysis in my area, funding options, and contacting more manufacturers. I was successfully able to secure a bank loan and then I knew I was in full preparation mode. My research time totally transformed my thought process and I was able to see the positive side of my setback. I needed to learn a lot more about this industry and market and how I could effectively excel within it. I was an outsider in an industry dominated by Asian business owners whose products were mostly manufactured over-seas and imported. Still, I was determined to succeed.

Towards the end of my disability period, I received medical clearance to return to work. Although physically I didn't feel ready due to residual pain and swelling, I did what was expected of me and informed my job of the doctor's report. That same day, I excit-edly waited for the arrival of a product catalogue from one of the largest hair product distributors which would further my expertise in the beauty industry. In my elation, I lost control of the package and of all the places it landed was on my healing broken toe. I was crushed in more ways than one — another painful hospital trip resulting in another setback to my job and business.

Over the weekend, I reflected on my tumultuous journey where I wavered between fulfilling my entrepreneurial ambitions and the stable career I had built. I was the bird perched at the end of the branch, with an opportunity right ahead of me. I interpreted the ironic repeat injury as a sign from God that this bird was meant to fly. Monday morning, I called HR to inform them of my deci-sion and she suggested I should take some time to think about it. I didn't need it and I told her as such. I already leaped and there was no going back. With that I submitted my official resignation letter, saying goodbye to my 9 to 5, and hello to entrepreneurship. Even though my company was in its infancy and more challenges laid ahead, I had become who I envisioned as a little girl. I was now a woman who lived life on her own terms, with outstretched arms and God beneath my wings.

On June 6, 2008, Big Apple Beauty Supply, Inc. opened its first location, and on October 13, 2013, a second location was opened in Pennsylvania. In 2017, we expanded yet again launching an online retail site BABShair.com. None of this was easy, but all of it was fulfilling. Through my business, I was able to execute my wishes to pour into my community. We organized scholarships for high school students, prom dresses for high school seniors, annual drives for back to school supplies and Thanksgiving meals for local families, a Christmas dinner for nursing home residents, and donated several wigs to the local American Cancer Society. These events came to garner approval and excitement from the community, but to me, I just felt privileged to be able to display my blessings to those around me.

From humble beginnings to operating in the beauty industry where according to the 2018 Nielsen Demographic Spending Report, African Americans spend more money while owning less than 20% of it, I overcame the odds. To own two physical and one online store in our community is rare, but through God's grace and mercy, I earned my place amongst an elite group of black-owned beauty supply store entrepreneurs. This was recognized and honored in 2018 when I received the prestigious 2018 Business Woman of the Year Award in Monroe County, PA.

I think about the woman I've become, and I am proud. A mother to two thriving sons, community agent and business owner living out her dreams. I hope that my journey can serve as a testimony that by believing in one's self and taking a leap of faith it is possible to LIFT, Launch and Lead through any circumstance.

> *"Now to Him who is able to do exceedingly abundantly above all that we ask or think, according to the power that works in us."*
>
> *~ Ephesians 3:20*

Count the Cost

By Chaundra Nicole Gore, MSL

Daily, throughout May 2016, I sat at my desk at the Army Reserve Medical Command G6 office in Pinellas Park, FL waiting patiently for my board results to Master Sergeant E8 in the United States Army. I watched the clock as the second hand went around numerous times until finally, 0800 hit. Yay! Congratulations were in order as my name was on the list with sequence number one. After being passed over for three years in a row, my time had arrived. This was truly a milestone that I dreamed of achieving for years. Super excited, I thanked God.

Months prior, I prayed persistently asking God to promote me, as I thought I was mentally and physically ready to take on a new challenge with more responsibility to excel. Little did I know it would come with a huge cost. After days of inhaling all the excitement and preparing for a huge party at my house and at my job, reality started to sink in. Questions started to come from my family and me. Would I be relocating and if so, how far away would it be? When would I have to move, and would my family be going with me? These were real questions that I needed to deal with and get answers to because my immediate concern was my family. As much as I was thankful for my promotion, I didn't want to move without my family.

Indeed, promotions do come from God, but in the Army, they are based on a need and how quickly they have to fill slots. The celebrations were over, the excitement had died, and now I had to face the hard reality of everything that involved my promotion to master sergeant. I prayed for the promotion, but I didn't pray to move or separate from my family and guess what, I was about to do both.

On June 1, 2016, I was promoted to Master Sergeant in the U.S. Army alongside two of my battle buddies. We had a huge luncheon and invited all our closest friends and family to attend. It was a day that I will never forget, but one thing was different. Everyone got to stay in place, but I had to move. Speaking with my management officer, I kept a close watch on my emails and phone to get the dreaded news of where I was headed. Fort Gordon, GA. Now that I had a location and a date to leave, the conversations and planning began with my family.

Four hundred thirty-five miles away, I could commute back and forth or take my family with me. I wanted everyone to go, but I had to talk it over with my husband and children to determine the best solution for us considering all the components of our household. My husband and I talked several times about our family's current circumstances. He has severe PTSD and was attending a local group therapy that suited him. He had also started a new job which he seemed to like. Our daughter Makiyah was preparing to have surgery to fix an abnormality on her heart. Our son Malik was facing a tumultuous season at school due to his battling adjust disorder and depression. Our youngest daughter was struggling with reading comprehension in school and so the roller coaster of emotions had begun for our family. What do we do? We decided to allow the family to stay temporarily until school got out. Faced with this decision I went ahead alone, and the journey began.

My plan was to pray and allow God to move in a mighty way to reunite us all, but it didn't go as intended. What seemed to be an adequate plan turned into my worst nightmare and a blessing at the same time. Hurdling days of loneliness and anxiety, I quickly focused on my job as an Army Reserve liaison to fill the void. Captivated with my new position, I got comfortable with where God placed me and blossomed right there. My boss became a great motivator who pushed me and gave me new challenges as I dealt with the routine business of solving problems for soldiers. It brightened my day and I looked forward to going into the office every morning at 0600. God blessed me with the gift of serving and I served the people that needed me the most at Fort Gordon—the Army Reserve soldiers.

From the beginning to the end of their training experience, I had the unique responsibility of making sure every soldier who arrived for training was in-processed and well taken care of. In addition, my sergeant major gave me a very special assignment to plan, prepare and implement the very first Army Reserve Birthday on Fort Gordon. I promptly assembled a team of five, collected information necessary to carry out the task, met weekly to plan, then executed a spectacular event. April 22, 2017, finally arrived, and we were ready. It was a celebration that would be captured by the Globe newspaper and talked about for months to come. This was an historic occasion that became a success with the generous help of my brothers and sisters in arms from Kappa Lambda

Chi, Military Fraternity Incorporated and Kappa Epsilon Psi Military Sorority Incorporated respectively. I was pleased to accomplish such a huge task, while simultaneously being worried about my family and running an office serving soldiers on a full-time basis.

Developing a deeper relationship with God got me through this difficult season. I learned to meditate every day although initially I could only sit still and focus for a minute or so. As I strategically created my war room in my apartment, God began to speak to my life, and I listened. A war room is a small space in your home that you create and go to whenever you are warring in the spirit and tapping into God's heavenly realm. I would put up sticky notes with affirmations, prayers, and words of encouragement to get me through each day. During this time, I was faced with the challenge of driving back and forth to see my family, sustain my marriage and watch over and support my children. It was so hard that I cried on most of my drives to and from because I was missing my family very much.

Thinking about how this was a self-inflicted wound, I tried always to see the best in the situation, but it wasn't enough to keep me from thinking about it. "When are they coming?" I asked myself quite a bit. Also, I questioned why my family had to go through this. I missed the daily love connection I had with them. My husband's condition got worse and he needed me, but I couldn't be there Monday through Friday. Although school was now out, because my husband's state of mind was an issue, we made a hard decision to delay even longer. This started a new set of challenges for me.

My time at Fort Gordon had allowed me to receive a basic housing allowance because I was separated from my family and

I was coming to the end of that allotted period. It was time for another waiver to get me through until the end of January. At the beginning of the new year, on January 2, 2018, my mother passed away which caused additional pain and turmoil for my family. She had been battling various health conditions and ultimately was placed on hospice care to be made comfortable until her demise. When this happened, I reflected upon all that she had done for me as my adoptive mother. My mom made sure I got what I needed out of life until I was able to take care of myself. Although it was a bittersweet and tumultuous time, I felt at peace and thought I had my emotions under control, but I really didn't.

Frankly, I didn't seek any help until I found myself under fire on my job, buried knee deep in a government accusation of defrauding the government. It was devastating. My boss kept asking me for documents to substantiate my case, documents I didn't have and so I reached out to someone who knew my case file really well for assistance. They told me everything would be okay and provided me with a document. That very document landed me in the Criminal Investigation Division office for questioning. As I sat waiting to be questioned, it felt like God came down from heaven and sat next to me to comfort me like no other. He told me to be still and know that He was there. He advised me to tell the truth and to know that I would be okay. Well, that's exactly what I did. The case didn't end until September with an outcome of me only getting extra duty, for which I was extremely grateful. It was a victory for me because it could have been far worse.

2018 was a year of testing, trials and tribulations for me. These various situations showed me my strength and weaknesses. They also gave me a stronger faith to lean on God and to trust Him. Just when I thought the tide was calming, my husband hit me with the news of wanting a divorce. Surprisingly, he informed me by text message—no call, no face to face but a text message. Clearly the enemy of my soul knew he couldn't get me through all the other things I faced, so he tapped into my husband. Feeling abandoned and lonely, he sought support and strength from another woman and decided to try to keep it a secret. I recognized this was yet another storm that would cause my faith to grow stronger. Furthermore, it would allow God to show Himself faithful once again.

Not only was I growing and standing on the word of God, but also my husband had been doing good, changing for the better. He was going to church, going fishing more often and enjoying things he loved, when all of a sudden, he became consumed with anger and guilt. My husband voiced his concerns about how he was being treated in our marriage and expressed that I wasn't listening to him. Admittedly, we made some mistakes that got us to that point.

We both made a conscious decision for me to go to Augusta alone (mistake #1) and though I traveled back and forth, I was also not giving my husband his needed time with me (mistake #2). Additionally, I allowed our children to basically exist and operate independently of parental guidance, not in a bad way, but it was happening (mistake #3). These were valid issues, but to me not enough to cause adultery. I had fixed mistake #2 back in May, but my husband was already blinded by the will of the enemy to see that change had already taken place. I eliminated the very thing he complained was taking my time—my sorority meetings. I knew God had a master plan and that was to bring me home for good, so I began to pray as if I was in a spiritual battle. This kept me calm, focused and poised to wait on God.

Without a doubt, I know no marriage is perfect, and you must work patiently at it. I do have my flaws, but all I asked of my husband was to wait until God brought me back home, and he couldn't do that. That's when I recognized I was dealing with generational curses and soul ties. God prepared me for it, and I went to work in the spiritual realm. Marriage takes two and we were both at fault for different reasons, but it also takes two to fix the issues of concern. Unfortunately, you can't fix anything if one has chosen to move on without you.

Given thirty days of leave to be home after having a hysterectomy, God revealed to me every detail about the turmoil in my marriage, abandonment, generational curse, and demonic spirits that were operating within my household. I put on my war clothes and I have been battling ever since. It doesn't matter what it looks like; it only matters what God said. My prayer is for God's will to be done in my life and for marriage restoration. With God leading me every step of the way, I choose to walk by faith and not by sight.

It's a daily choice to live by my beliefs while learning to be more mindful of the cost of my decisions. Being able to count the cost of a situation is very essential. Often times, we make decisions based on what we see right now, instead of thinking ahead and weighing the options. As my pastor, Dr. Jomo Cousins, said, "Life is based on decisions and consequences. The choices you make will cost you." Indeed, this is very true.

Those storms I went through either cost me money, time, effort, peace of mind, my joy, or sleep. Although they strengthened me and made me draw closer to God, I didn't count the cost of my decisions before-hand. From my experiences, I learned that when we contemplate the cost of a situation, we would be inclined to make better decisions and realize that some of them are not worth the trouble. I further understand that when we place a high value especially on our loved ones, we will consider the impact our decisions have on them. We cannot take that lightly.

Before you make a decision that may cost you everything, I challenge each of you to pause, ponder, and pray. Don't be hasty! Consult wise counsel and stop talking to people who have never walked the path in which you are trying to go. Let God guide you. I am grateful He took me through my storms, gave me the promotion I prayed fervently for, challenged my decision-making abilities under fire, allowed turmoil to pass through His hands to my marriage, and rescued me in the time of trouble despite the fact that I didn't fully consider my actions. God is faithful, and I pray that my story has encouraged you in one way or another to count your cost before you make any decisions.

Be Blessed!

Freedom in the Fire

By Melissa Castro-Wilson

" **I** f any one of you tries to leave, I will kill you," are words I will never forget. As if it happened moments ago, I still remember the look in his eyes, the blank stare that stood out amidst the darkness in the room, letting us know he was very angry. That anger resonated in the tone of his voice, one filled with rage and an outright fear-inducing sound that travelled throughout the house. With tears streaming down my face, the fear I felt that night caused a gut-wrenching knot in my stomach as my stepfather sat cross-legged in front of our apartment door. We were trapped and at his mercy. You see, that night he had come home tripping off a bad high of heroin, and we knew we were in for a long night. My mom desperately tried to reason with him hoping he would let us leave but he refused, and so we stood there, paralyzed by the fear that gnawed away at us while waiting for him to either fall asleep or come down from this terrible high. It was dreadful and I really did think I was going to die.

Sadly, that night can be considered a semi-typical story for where I come from. I grew up in the South Bronx, one of the poorest neighborhoods in New York City. It was in the epicenter of the heroin crisis and so drugs were a part of our everyday lives. Our neighborhood was so bad there were streets you knew you could not walk through because they were completely occupied by addicts panhandling or selling items to get their next fix. The struggle to survive and thrive in an environment filled with poverty, drug addiction and fatherlessness was literally a fight for one's life.

As a child, I witnessed the distribution of drugs, and on one occasion I even found myself caught in the middle of a crossfire between police and the local drug dealers and had to hide beneath a parked car. It was an all-out fight for my life! Stories like these made you want to run for your life, and on one occasion we had to do just that in the middle of the night because of gunshots being fired into my neighbor's apartment door. It turned out the individual who was the intended target wasn't even home. These are not things you can easily forget, and so I buried them and made a promise to myself that one day I would make sure that I "got out."

I can't tell you how my mother met my stepfather; I just know he was always there. When he was sober, he was an amazing dad and I loved him very much, but when he relapsed, it was absolute hell. My mom desperately tried to help him get clean and was an active participant in drug rehab programs, interventions and lots of visits to see him in jail. It was a life that also included coming home to our apartment emptied out on several occasions because he had sold all our belongings for his next fix. For about 15 years, we endured many long nights like the one I described, but this one was by far the worst and it had a tremendous impact on me and who I was to become.

I realized later in life that this incident and many like it taught me that living a life filled with trauma and chaos was normal because it was what I had experienced for so long. Many of the choices I went on to make as an adult were the direct result of the negative experiences from my past. Growing up, we lived on public assistance and supplemental disability due to medical ailments that did not afford my mother the ability to work. She did the best she could with what she had, and I don't ever remember going hungry or lacking the bare essentials. My mom made sure my sister and I were well taken care of but emotionally, she was fighting her own battles, so I had to grow up way too fast. I found myself in relationships where I was never respected, taken advantage of and even outright abused. Consequently, my decisions caused me lots of heartache and pain.

At the tender age of seventeen, I became pregnant with my first child, my precious daughter Destiny who taught me the true meaning of love. Many around me thought my life was ruined when they found out, that I, a teenager, would soon have a child of my own. But she was by far one of the best things that ever happened to me. I worked diligently and graduated valedictorian of my high school class with my three-month-old daughter in the crowd. It was one of the proudest moments of my life. Her dad and I were two young kids trying to be responsible; however, we were naive about what we had just gotten ourselves into. The relationship eventually ended amicably as we were young and lost and had no idea how to make it last.

After my daughter's father and I went our separate ways, I tried to bond with other men, but those relations also failed. It was a challenge for me to have successful relationships because of my childhood trauma. As a child, I never felt validated, nor did I feel I had a voice. No matter how out of control situations were in my home, my input was never taken into consideration because I was just a "child" and did not understand "adult" situations. My entire life, I always felt like I had to prove my worth to receive the approval of others and so that behavior followed me into my romantic relationships. Whether with my ex-husband or my children's dads, I lacked the self-respect and self-love required to set firm boundaries in how I deserved to be treated. I lacked the will power to say no to behaviors that went against every moral standard I held close to my heart. Regrettably, I allowed myself to be disrespected on every level imaginable.

From verbal abuse to emotional and physical abuse, I have experienced them all. I have been lied to, cheated on and physically hit at the hands of men that were supposed to love, honor, cherish and protect me. I found myself in relationships doomed to fail from the very beginning, yet I stayed because I believed if I loved hard enough, if I was a good enough partner, if I forgave enough then maybe, just maybe, they would change. All the while what I was doing was sacrificing myself, my health and my sanity in the hopes of being loved in whatever shape or form it was being offered, even at the expense of myself. Of course, at the time I didn't realize I was settling for scraps when I deserved nothing but the very best. Now, as I have learned to love and accept myself, I have also learned what healthy relationships should entail.

Those life lessons from my relationships didn't come easy. I had to ask myself some really difficult questions about what I wanted my life to look like going forward. I have had to do plenty of hard work on myself as I realize that there are many unhealthy patterns that have been consistent throughout my entire life. I know now that I have nothing to prove to anyone but myself and that the common denominator in every single one of those failed relationships was me. Therefore, I must face my past, face my pain, face the rejection that has kept me bound and walk in the freedom that God has already granted me by sacrificing His life on the cross. This has been very challenging, and I have struggled to learn how to forgive myself, love myself, and embrace the individual I have been predestined to become by God.

Although I have forgiven those individuals for their behaviors, as a single woman, I truly have struggled to forgive myself for allowing such horrendous treatment in my life. In hindsight, I realize what I endured as a child inevitably affected my decisions. Much of the trauma I suffered in my past and what I also watched my mother experience at the hands of my abusive step-father were repeated in my life because it's what I had been exposed to growing up. It was learned behavior and the patterns were already laid out for me to follow, which I did without a second thought. But when I found myself at rock bottom, I found the rock at the bottom, Christ, my healer, my redeemer and my strength, who had already forgiven me for it all.

It wasn't until I found myself in the fetal position crying out in desperation for an answer to why I've had to endure so much pain in my life that God stepped in like the gentle Father that He is. When my entire world fell apart, not by choice, but because of decisions made by someone else, I finally surrendered my life to the One who holds the solution to every single problem I will ever encounter on this side of heaven. I was exhausted from running the race of self-sufficiency, self-reliance, self-will and every other self that exists in the dictionary. My life had spiraled completely out of control and I was now a single mother to a teenager and a young adult. Lost, broken and extremely afraid, I did not like what my life had become, who I had become and where this journey had brought me, and so I cried out to God. Somehow, by God's grace and mercy, I had to pick myself up off the floor and move forward no matter what that looked like or how tough it would be.

BUT GOD!! He saved me. He pursued me. He set me free! He met me in my brokenness and gently pushed me on the journey towards healing and wholeness, all the while strategically providing me with a community of people at The FLOW Kingdom Ministries, that would support me and give me the tough love I needed to face my pain no matter how difficult or scary it might be. In all the trauma, the sadness, and the pain, in all the moments where I felt rejected, hopeless, overwhelmed and afraid, God was there. He is the reason why I am still standing and why I have survived every single trauma I have faced throughout my entire life. It has all been for a greater purpose, but it would be easy for someone who doesn't understand His ways to question why God would allow so much adversity, so much sadness, and so much loss. However, when we learn to understand that He did not cause it, but He can and will use it for our greater good, then we can truly heal.

I see now that every trial by fire, every tribulation, every single valley I have ever faced was all strategically orchestrated to assist me in finding my purpose to be a voice for broken women who have lost themselves along the way, to be a voice for those who have never, ever felt heard, loved or accepted. It is because of every single tear that I have ever cried that the desire to equip and empower women of diverse backgrounds to walk in their purpose was birthed. My intention is to teach women how to love, honor, and value themselves all the while chasing after their God-given dreams. It is my mission to establish a community in which women can express their love for one another and for Christ all the while giving back to the world around them. Furthermore, my desire is to foster a community where women can grow spiritually, physically, mentally and financially, to encourage a safe place where everyone is welcomed and where they will know there is room for every single one of us to thrive, to live, and to excel in our God-given gifts and abilities.

When we can finally get to the place where collaboration replaces competition, then we will be able to appreciate that we are all uniquely created by God with specific gifts and talents to support each other. It is my heart's desire for women to understand that their identity and worth is found in Christ and that no one else but Him can ever satisfy the void we have deep within us. As I continue to live my life out loud, I want others to see that what Satan tried so hard to use as weapons of mass destruction, God has used as tools in my re-construction and it is because of what I have endured that I can now stand with my head held high, not as a victim but as a victorious warrior who has found her freedom in the midst of the fire. In this fire, I continue to be refined, no longer consumed by trauma because I am far too immersed in His love.

This amazing love holds the solution to everything I have ever faced. It is not my distorted idea of love based on what I had learned along the way, but Christ's love that has truly set me free. His love has healed the wounds and mended my broken heart. This very love has transformed me, equipped me and empowered me to continue running the race set before me. Although I cannot say I am grateful for the pain, I am extremely thankful for what I have gained along the way, my freedom, my faith, and my foundation in the One who holds me in the palm of His hand. The One who promises that no matter what I face, He will always be with me and He will always hear me, love me, protect me and cherish me. It is His love that has brought me to my knees and the very same love that has called me redeemed, chosen, daughter, beloved, and friend.

A Wealthy Me

By Khalima Green

People often have a misconception about being wealthy, thinking it is just money, but wealth is a lifestyle. It is a choice to be better and wiser emotionally, spiritually, physically and financially. All components of wealth are important. They go hand in hand and a balance is needed, yet, it's most essential to be well-balanced on the emotional side to enjoy the other parts of being wealthy. Suffering from any emotional trauma can have a terrible effect on everything else in life and, in some shape or form, we all have experienced it. Most often, we have not fully dealt with the situation or we allow it to take control of our lives. However, overcoming emotional pain is vital for anyone who desires to live an authentic lifestyle of wealth.

Emotional healing is a process that takes time, strength, and a lot of courage. The work itself is an investment with great returns, more valuable than money. When I went through my traumatic experience, I discovered a blueprint that can help anyone to overcome an emotional hurdle. As I navigated my way out of a dark and depressed time in my life, I used four steps to come to my peaceful place of a wealthy me and to find my calling along the way.

Out of the blue, my husband shocked me with the news that

he wanted a divorce. Within a week of being told he wanted out of our marriage, I found out I was pregnant, and miscarried for the third time. Then, six weeks later, when we were supposed to be separated, I discovered that I was pregnant again. I felt foolish and hurt. As I questioned myself and wondered why I placed myself in a position to get pregnant again, I immediately thought to myself maybe things can change, so I decided to fight for my marriage.

The first thing I did was to pray and fast before God and saturate the room he was sleeping in with holy oil. I also took the initiative to go for counseling and was excited when he agreed to let our Pastor and her husband counsel us. I even allowed myself to be more vulnerable, which was big for me because I am not a mushy person. I was certain this was going to help us restore our marriage. Unfortunately, I was wrong. It got worse! Everything I tried did not move him. My husband had shut down on me. I was so upset and did not know what to do anymore.

Meanwhile, with all that was going on, I had returned to college and was doing well, earning A's and B's to obtain my bachelor's in business management. Everything looked good on the outside, but it was hell at home. We argued behind closed doors and he was no longer discreet about his secrets. I could not believe this was the same man who I had exchanged vows with and who said he loved me. Now he acted like I meant nothing to him and did not even acknowledge my pregnancy. As much as I wanted my marriage, I refused to be disrespected. Filled with anger, I wanted him out my house, and yes, I said my house because I wasn't going anywhere. He set a date to leave, but I wanted him out ASAP. It was time for him to move out my way just like he had said himself.

Eventually, he left, but my heart yearned for him. I was an emotional wreck, crying all the time; I even cried myself to sleep. One day, I was experiencing morning sickness, and while I had my head in the toilet bowl vomiting and crying, my mother in law showed up to console me. I'll never forget that morning, because boy, did that make me angry. Moments like that were difficult for me since I still wanted my husband. I wanted him to take care of me. I wanted us to experience this parenting journey together. I did not want to be a single mother again. I pleaded with God, "what did I do to deserve this?" "He asked me to work on myself, and I did just that," "Please God, take the pain away because I don't want to feel this pain anymore." I wanted to be loved and nurtured by my husband, so I waited a while to see if he would return. After a year, reality hit me, and I realized he wasn't coming back. I knew then I had to move on from the relationship and focus on my boys.

Even though I didn't get my happily ever after fairy tale ending, my desire for a successful marriage came from a pure place. Growing up, I was adamant about being married. See, I grew up in a multi-generational family household. My grandmother took care of my siblings and me while my mother worked to provide a great lifestyle for us. I watched the women (mother, grandmother and aunt) in my life be strong, independent, single women who did every and anything necessary to take care of their kids with or without a man. They lived life well, but I wanted to break the generational curse of a single parent household and experience the blessing of marriage. I was so happy to be the first out of nine grandchildren to get married that I never imagined I'd be a disappointment and divorced at 33.

My divorce was incredibly painful. However, with a renewed mind, I decided not to let my past dictate my life. I regained control over my life with the help and strength of God. He gave me mercy, favor and grace to get through the trauma and grow from it. I forgave myself, forgave my ex-husband, and found peace in the Lord as I declared myself to be the Proverbs 31 woman. She is many things, and I am her; God-fearing, businesswoman, hard worker, faithful, mother, wife and more. Yes, I said WIFE! I have not given up on marriage, and I believe the Father is preparing MY HUSBAND. So, while God prepares this man of valor, I have continued to focus on motherhood, my calling and career.

Professionally, I was excelling in my career, but I needed God to reveal my ministry to me. I always had a passion to help and be an advocate for women, so I asked God what group of Your daughters do You want me to minister to and what do I minister to them? I fasted, prayed and stayed still to receive a word, then one day, it occurred on me. Somehow, I noticed women who were going through divorces or just recently divorced were constantly coming across my path. There would be times when they would ask various questions about what the divorce process entailed. Women wanted information on the fees, lawyers and simply how to get through it. I had the knowledge they were seeking and was willing to provide them the answers. This was my ministry starting to unfold.

I would never forget being at a retreat and during the meet and greet time, the Spirit of the Lord directed my path to a young lady He wanted me to speak to. Honestly, I was disobedient and did not talk to her. Instead, I continued to mingle with everyone else. Finally, on the last day, I approached her and introduced myself (the Spirit of God insisted). We were having a wonderful conversation when she asked me a question. Instantly as I answered, tears rolled down her face and she said, "Thank you, do you know how many other people I asked the same question and the way you explained it to me, I understand and receive it." Her response led me to ask if she was married and when she answered, "I'm divorced," all I could say in my mind was WOW! CONFIRMATION! I knew without a doubt this was my calling.

A year later, I finally decided to launch my coaching business as a Transitional Divorce Coach to help divorced women regain their confidence and to become a wealthy version of themselves, emotionally and spiritually first and financially afterward. To assist them through their transition, I designed a blueprint called, "A Wealthy Me." This tool provides guidance to evolve into a healthier and wealthier you. It shows women that wealth is more than money. Indeed, it is having an abundance of valuable resources which God, who is the Most High, has provided already for us. Everything starts in the soul and a wealthy soul is powerful. In fact, the scripture says, "Beloved, I wish above all things that you may prosper and be in health even as your soul prospers" (3 John 2). When women gain the knowledge and apply this blueprint to overcome their divorce, their lives will be supernaturally transformed, spiritually and physically.

"A WEALTHY ME" BLUEPRINT"

SEEK: Asking for help can be hard, especially if you feel stressed or confused. However, getting the support you need during tough times can help you get through the situation, give you strategies to deal with it and give you a new perspective.

Spiritually

Seek God's counsel for whatever situation you're facing. God does not want you to do it alone. Talk to Him and tell Him your problems; cry to Him. Lay everything down at His feet. Yearn for His attention. *"Cast your burden on the Lord, and He shall sustain you; He shall never permit the righteous to be moved"* (Psalm 55:22).

When you seek God's counsel and make it a constant habit, this will build your trust and a bond with the Lord. As you establish this relationship, it will allow Him to intervene in your life.

Physically

You're also going to need to seek a good circle of support – friends, family, pastor, professional counseling and accountability partners.

Example: As I mentioned, my divorce was a traumatic experience. To get through it, I prayed to God every day asking Him to heal my bleeding heart and to help me understand. Not only was I able to vent to the Lord, but also, I had supportive friends and family that provided love and support. In addition, I sought professional counseling.

PURGE: Purging is preparation for the next level. This is an emotionally painful process, and sometimes it comes with tremendous pressure. Think of it as a detox, to get the hurt out while you renew your mind and spirit. Be sure to allow yourself to cry. Crying is very important and is naturally purifying as you transition for the better.

Spiritually

Now that you have cast your cares upon the Lord, allow Him to purge you which simply is allowing God to get rid of impurities in your heart. The Holy Spirit will begin to reveal things to you that aren't right about what you've been thinking or doing that He wants out of your life. *"Purge me with hyssop and I shall be clean; wash me and I shall be whiter than snow"* (Psalm 51:7).

Physically

Clean your house. You cannot mix the old and the new meaning old ways must go, which include toxic relationships, bad eating habits, harmful behaviors, negative thought patterns and poor choices.

Example: After I asked God to heal my bleeding heart, He began revealing my ways to me such as behaviors that I had done intentionally and unintentionally. He wanted to cleanse me of them. Because these revelations hurt, He provided comfort in my trying time. I took it day by day while adjusting to the change. Daily, I made it a habit to read the Word. And I cried. God had shown me my ugly and although I did not like it, I had to accept the truth.

ACKNOWLEDGE: Now that you know how to seek and establish a relationship with God, and you also understand that you must allow Him to purge you, it is time to acknowledge the decisions you made in your life. Everyone plays a role in every situation. Yes, some things are out of your control, but in other circumstances, you must take ownership. This is the growth stage.

Spiritually

Pay attention to what God is showing you. After He reveals the truth, you must be ready to be accountable for your actions. *"In all your ways acknowledge him and he shall direct your path"* (Proverbs 3:6).

Physically

Have you acknowledged the decisions you made? Have you acknowledged your behaviors?

Example: I had to acknowledge a few things in my life. First, I reflected on the relationship I had with my oldest son's father and had to admit it was unhealthy. My son and I deserved better; still, it took me two years to leave. Second, I had to acknowledge the wrong behavior I displayed in my marriage.

My ex-husband was very kind with his words and he never spoke harsh to me, yet my words were harsh. I had to acknowledge my role and admit the marriage was over. Things happen. I cannot control everything and, I cannot control anybody.

ACTIVATE: After you get through the steps of seeking God, letting Him purge you, examining yourself, and acknowledging your role in the situation, it is now time for you to ACTIVATE.

Spiritually
"Then He touched their eyes, saying, "According to your faith let it be to you" (Matthew 9:29), meaning become what you believe. In other words, activate what you believe!

Physically
Take everything you learned and apply it. Take initiative to transform your life. Practice new behaviors and make better decisions.

Example: I moved on from my ex-husband and started to pursue the things I liked. I wanted to change my words and attitude, so I spoke softer. Furthermore, I desired to travel, so I found ways to make it happen. Most importantly, I found my calling and activated it by becoming a Transitional Divorce Coach.

ACTIVATION! This is your moment to become a healthier version of you emotionally, spiritually, physically and financially with emphasis on the emotional aspect of your being. Deal with situations that may be holding you back; take back your life as I took back mine. By the grace of God, it took four years to change my life around, and if He can do it for me, He most certainly can do it for you as well.

I pray "A Wealthy Me" blueprint will give you a better perspective about the circumstances you are facing. It is designed for you to apply these steps to almost any situation. The process will take time and everyone's situation is different; however, it is possible to heal from emotional trauma and live a wealthy lifestyle.

Closed Mouths Don't Get Fed

By Cheray Diggs

"When you stand and share your story in an empowering way, your story will heal you and your story will heal somebody else." ~ Iyanla Vanzant

Whether you're using written or verbal communication, it's important to know how to express yourself so others can fully understand the intent of your message. This is an essential skill to have, yet it did not come to me easily. The ability to communicate is an art that's developed over time. For years, I was afraid to write much less speak up about what I desired in my life. It was a journey of self-discovery to find my voice as I needed to unlearn specific behaviors from my childhood. By the grace of God and with the support of a therapist, I realized that silencing my voice was unhealthy, plus it kept me from receiving the things I wanted in life.

Growing up, we weren't allowed to question authority nor were we allowed to speak up for ourselves. I lived in a "do as I say" household. My mom laid down the rules, and we did as we were told. She did not have time to sit and discuss anything, not even the facts of life when I entered puberty. Friends and certain family members taught me about personal hygiene, sex, and relationships among other things. They answered the questions I had, and I quietly figured out the rest on my own.

From childhood, I learned early how to take care of me the best way I could. Even though I knew my parents loved me, they were so busy with other family matters that I barely received attention from them. I was the child who didn't give them any trouble. Thus they basically left me on my own. Little did my parents know how much I needed them to nurture me and make me feel special.

At home, I did not feel like I fit in, so I grew up with low self-worth. I also would observe that the men got the attention while the women were expected to be submissive to them. The unspoken code was the women should be seen and not heard, which was the way my mother interacted with my father. Their relationship was totally dysfunctional, but I didn't recognize it at the time. Mom was always working hard to make everything right, but she would allow all the credit to go to my dad even though he was laid back and didn't do much. As I got older, my mother's actions led me to believe that I should put myself behind others and shy away from receiving praises for my achievements.

My perception of my parents' relationship along with not being allowed to speak up at home impacted how I interacted with people, especially men. I always believed it was normal to settle for less when dating and to cater to the needs of my male friends while neglecting my own desires. Actually, I didn't have the courage or self-confidence to speak up; I had no voice. It was etched in my mind that my thoughts and opinions did not matter.

Finding my voice was a journey filled with anxiety that affected every area of my life. I even had a fear of asking anyone for help because I didn't want to be indebted to others. As my apprehensions took a toll, I decided it was time to make some changes. I was frustrated with both my personal and romantic relationships. They were not working; in fact, most were draining. I had allowed people to take advantage of my kindness partly because I longed for them to like me. My inability to confront others and talk about my feelings led me to a dark place.

Depression was now sitting on me. I was tired of feeling like people were using me and taking my kindness for weakness, but it wasn't their fault. Primarily, the problem was me. Having low self-image and equally low self-esteem made it difficult for others to treat me well since I didn't even know how to treat myself in a loving manner. Eventually, I sought counseling to help me navigate some of these issues that were complicating my life.

Although therapy is not discussed openly and considered taboo in the black community, I knew it was necessary for my well-being. Seeing a professional counselor was a major step in my healing and finding my voice. At first, it was hard because I was not ready for some of the feedback my therapist gave me. She made assessments that forced me to take an honest look at myself to unpack all my baggage. Patiently, she assisted me in sorting out such issues as people pleasing to be accepted, not standing up for myself, letting people disrespect me, and not loving myself. Each therapy session gave me insight into who I was and who I would become at the end.

For many years, I went to therapy but only discussed it with my mom, a few friends and certain family members. It wasn't for everybody else to know because I felt they wouldn't understand how much my therapist was helping me. She taught me a lot about myself and interestingly, even though we have different cultural backgrounds, we still could relate to each other. Through therapy, I gained strength to stand up for myself and to say no when I didn't want to do something. I also discovered how to love myself more than I love others. Before, I would put others ahead of myself, but now it's God first, myself next and others last. Also, I learned how to handle criticism. So, if I think people are being critical, instead of getting upset, I'm able to accept their comments and apply the advice to improve my life.

Therapy did wonders for me. It helped me through several crises over the years. The loss of my mother in January 2015 really challenged my faith and my relationships. It took me a while to deal with the sorrow I felt and was thankful that my therapist assisted me in processing my grief. The next challenge was when I lost my job in November 2016 after working with EmblemHealth for 24 years. Again, my therapist was there to guide me through that loss which was very upsetting. She was a great support to manage my emotions, so I wouldn't fall into depression and go into isolation.

Her counsel changed my belief system about myself and gave me a new perspective on how to cope with my problems. It also impacted my relationships because some people don't appreciate the new me, since the old Cheray who would tolerate their nonsense is gone. I've lost friendships and family members, but I stand strongly in my belief that my happiness comes first. I love myself and am delighted about the new me who is no longer afraid to express herself. My therapy sessions allowed me to discover my voice and take charge of my life.

Along with therapy, other resources I used to find solutions for my issues were self-help books. They gave me information that guided me to develop boundaries in my relationships, to disconnect from negative and dysfunctional people, and to say "No" without feeling guilty. Those books were very useful, but I also needed my Bible. It played a very important part to changing my life as I incorporated God in my world while I was getting healthier mentally and emotionally. The spiritual aspect was very important to my growth and to me being who I am today.

Adding the spiritual component was so powerful because it made me understand that God loved me in my recovery and He already forgave me for all the mistakes I made in the past. My relationship with God was a tremendous help to unlearn wrong beliefs and renew my mind. In the process, I joined a church to be around other believers and that also blessed me. Having a strong connection to my heavenly Father plus therapy and the books was a great combination for me to become the woman that He wanted me to be. The grace of God made a significant difference for me to truly overcome my childhood issues.

I would encourage anyone who needs to sort out their problems to seek help from a therapist, read books and establish an intimate relationship with God. Yes, it was a hard decision to go to counseling, but it was one of the best choices I ever made. I honestly think sometimes we need an outside person to listen as we talk out our problems because the people that are close to us can't be objective. They mean well, but their knowledge of us will get in the way when we try to work through personal difficulties. Seeing someone to listen and give us feedback on how to handle our challenges won't bring instant changes, but with faith and persistence, life will get better as we apply what we are learning.

It's an investment in yourself to get help, so do something to improve your self-esteem and take baby steps because, in the end, you matter. My friend used to tell me she noticed that God always removes people from my life, and she's right; I've lost a lot of people that held no purpose in my journey. It took work, years and determination but I'm glad I did put in the effort. My heart is grateful for this journey of self-awareness and for the self-confidence that God has given me by way of therapy.

I realized during those times when I felt alone, He was constantly there by my side. It's heartwarming to know that my journey was not in vain and that it will help someone else. I've learned that women must speak up with confidence for themselves. My motto, "Closed mouths don't get fed" means we must speak in authority and whatever we want, if we don't open our mouths, we won't get it. As women, we must speak what we desire into existence. The other meaning of that motto is not to be fearful of asking people for help when you need it.

Through my walk of faith and quest to self-love, I hope my motto of "Closed mouths don't get fed" resonates in your own personal journey, trials and tribulations. We all need support in this walk called "Life" and remember, God can use anyone and anything to assist you in overcoming issues affecting your destiny. Therefore, step out on your faith and let it take you farther than you could ever imagine. Take all the opportunities to change your life, knowing the world is your oyster!

Moving to the Heart of the Matter

By Vanessa I. Farrell

*Thirty women will be dead
before you complete this chapter!*

Every single minute of every single day, a woman dies as a result of heart disease, stroke, or another form of cardiovascular disease (CVD). That totals 1,440 women each day. These are real people like you and me. They are our daughters, sisters, wives, aunts, mothers, and best friends. Every woman is at risk of CVD just by being a female.

So why aren't we outraged about the 1,440 women who died yesterday and those who will die today and tomorrow as a result of CVD? Imagine that each day, three 747 passenger planes crashed, killing everyone on board. Not only would people be leery of getting on a plane ever again, but if this happened, all flights would be grounded until the source of the problem was identified and rectified. We would undoubtedly get to the heart of the matter.

A very common condition of heart disease is high blood pressure (HBP), known as "the silent killer" because those who suffer from it usually don't show any symptoms. Typically, many HBP victims walk around feeling normal, completely unaware of the ticking time bomb that can devastate their lives. Then, there are those diagnosed with the condition who don't do the right things to maintain a healthy lifestyle and manage their blood pressure. They often fall into bad habits, such as:

- Not monitoring blood pressure and "hoping it will disappear."
- Eating foods that raise blood pressure "because they taste good."
- Not taking medication because "it makes me feel funny."
- Saying they're *blessed*, but if truth be told, God knows they are s-t-r-e-s-s-e-d out and too afraid or ashamed to confess it.

I have experienced this first-hand, walking around not knowing I was on the verge of becoming a statistic. Without warning, my blood pressure soared from normal (120/80) to as high as 195/110. When I realized what was happening, I was scared to death by this development – a clear indication that something was dangerously wrong.

The seams of my tidy existence began to unravel after I endured the harrowing experiences of two Category 5 hurricanes in 2017. I had just relocated to St. Croix in the US Virgin Islands after being away for almost 30 years and was elated to have landed a job there in the public health field. This was a dream come true. It had always been a career goal to work in public health either within an organization that was outside the contiguous 48 states or internationally. As such, I was over the moon when things fell into place.

Although I had moved numerous times before, resettling to the Caribbean was different. This time it was God-ordained. The motivation to relocate began percolating in mid-2015 with a still, small voice whispering, "You should move." At times, it came in wave-like emotions where I felt "washed over" and consumed. Also, there were instances when I would see, hear, or read things that reinforced the command. In addition, I had moments when I found myself immersed in this vision of moving and wondered if I was hallucinating.

The amazing thing about this experience was that I didn't know where I would be going. I began telling myself that I was heading to Florida to be closer to my sister and her family, especially since my dear mom had been there for some months recuperating and I had been traveling back and forth to Florida from Philadelphia quite often to visit her. Figuring out details of my move brought about a great deal of internal dialogue that made me question my sanity and provided a laundry list of what I'd be sacrificing. I'd have to sell my home of 10 years, leave my friends, resign from my employment of 12 years, and give up a great salary. I'd have to relinquish the known for the unknown. And I would do all this at 47 years old. Crazy as it sounds, I said yes to it all.

Amid all the swirling thoughts, I clearly heard God reaffirming His command, and He also stated, "Keep this close because most people would not understand." This was the hardest part of the journey, but I remained obedient and did not share this with many people. I felt like I was heading out on a journey without a destination. Through it all, I vowed to trust God.

Despite the anticipated loss I would endure from selling my home, I started the listing process. Then I began to detach myself from my home and my belongings. I didn't want to find myself loving my house or my things so much that I got stuck. My heart was fixed to sell what I could and give away the rest.

The most enlightening part of the process was when I was led to create a vision board. This was a very powerful exercise because it allowed me to actually see the vision that I had created and the obedience, faith, and intention I had exercised and to consider how everything placed on that vision board fell into place. On the board, I asked the Lord for four things:

- Help me sell my home!
- Allow me to have an amicable separation from my employer and friends.
- Increase my "territory" and help me find a job in public health (I had recently read The Prayer of Jabez).
- Prepare the right mate for me. I am open to God's provision.

So, here's what happened. My house sold in one day. The announcement of my departure from my job was met with love, enthusiasm, and celebration with co-workers and friends. Also, I got a position as a Territorial Director within the public health field. I'm still trusting in God's timing to deliver my mate; I know he's on the way! This experience taught me to always trust God, even when things are uncertain, to do my part and let God do the rest, to not force an outcome, and to have faith in God to handle the details.

After I applied for and obtained the position as the Territorial Director of the Communicable Diseases Division within the US Virgin Islands Health Department, I moved to St. Croix. This was nowhere on my radar. I had left St. Croix almost three decades ago, three months shy of the island being struck by Hurricane Hugo in September 1989. Now I returned, anticipating a new, more fulfilling life.

Fast forward four months. The US Virgin Islands were hit by two back-to-back Category 5 hurricanes in a two-week span. It was like being unexpectedly whiplashed while blindfolded. St. Thomas and St. John were first hit by Hurricane Irma on September 6, 2017. Irma devastated the islands, leaving thousands homeless. Only two weeks later, on September 20, Hurricane Maria tore through St. Croix, destroying people's livelihoods, property, and sense of security.

Following the hurricanes, work demands ballooned, and I was maxed out. The building that housed the clinic I managed was evacuated because of mold infestation resulting from storm damage. We provided clinical services in a tent, which offered little or no privacy. To make matters worse, I was charged with finding a new clinic space at a time when any commercial property left standing came at a premium. Needless to say, my stress level was mounting at work, while I went home to a house that was without running water for weeks and without electricity for 96 days.

I was in survival mode, lacking life's basic necessities once taken for granted. I could not cook proper meals, connecting to the outside world was challenging, and cell phone service was often spotty or non-existent. In retrospect, the scenes were comical, but at the time, all of this was necessary. People would camp out in lawn chairs at the few free Wi-Fi spots on the island to connect with their friends and families around the world. I would never have imagined having to drive across town to make a phone call, but I did.

During the months following the hurricanes, the environment no longer supported a healthy lifestyle. There were curfews, road closures, no street lighting, and no banking. Our economy became a cash economy. Fresh fruits and vegetable were scarce while packaged and processed foods were limitless. In fact, there was an endless supply of MREs (meals ready to eat). We were simply living and trying to cope in recovery mode. When I look back wondering how I made it, I know it was God who gave me strength each day. He provided my day's supply of grace, wisdom, and protection, and that's all I needed.

As the stress increased on the job, I did nothing to preserve my mental health. I was unaware of the compounding factors that were causing my anxiety level to rise. Through it all, I never missed a day of work. I went to work each day and, eight hours later, retreated to my dark house, only to repeat the process for more than three months.

Through the darkness, by the grace of God, hope arrived! Sheer joy consumed me when my neighborhood was energized on Sunday, December 24, 2017. It was the best Christmas gift I had ever received. I got back from church to a home where the refrigerator was humming, lights came on at the flip of a switch, and fans and air conditioner units were working. I could *finally* take a hot shower and a warm bath. The things I once took for granted were now priceless luxuries. I looked around the room teary-eyed, grateful to God for His protection during the last three months of darkness.

Then without warning, my wake-up call came on January 20, 2018, six months after the storms. I walked out of my doctor's office with a prescription in hand. My blood pressure was way too high, and I needed to be on medication. I was very sad that I found myself in this state. Although it wasn't the end of the world, my pride kicked in. I had always felt good about being the model of good health, a champion for wellness, the health degree holder, the certified health coach, and the master health education specialist. I was devastated.

How could this happen to me? I didn't want to be that person. I ate properly before the hurricane, so how could three months of bad habits override years of healthy eating? I was physically active and at a healthy weight and did not have a family history of high blood pressure. What on earth was going on with me? Clearly, what was going was I did not manage my stress and I threw my body out of whack by eating crap. I was having panic attacks throughout the day and waking up each morning on the verge of exhaustion, just thinking about the demands of the impending work day. I was stressed out working within a system that I had no control over. I loved the work but hated the job. I began asking myself if this is truly my calling or is it a sentence.

With the help of God, I knew I had the knowledge to restore my health, so I kicked into gear and went back to the basics. I knew exactly what my body needed to be whole. I began eating healthy, stopped eating packaged, processed foods, and began exercising. I was determined to heal my body. Despite my reluctance, I took the medication because I wanted my blood pressure to normalize. Then I made the ultimate decision. About a year and a half after starting my dream career, I *quit*. My dream had become a nightmare, so I woke up and quietly walked away.

Throughout this experience, I would earnestly seek God with all my heart for a turnaround. I continuously prayed, "Father, I know the God I serve. I know you would not have brought me to St. Croix to abandon me. I know you have a plan in place for my life that is much grander than I can conceive. I trust you." Personally, I didn't see a way out, but I kept praying and believing that God would open doors. They say God helps those who help themselves, but I wasn't even looking for or asking around about jobs. To be honest, I did not know where to begin looking, but praise be to God, an opportunity found me.

It was serendipitous. A former colleague called and offered me a position with her company with the ability to work remotely. It was unexpected but timely, and I truly believed that was God in action. He promised never to leave or forsake us, and I'm a living testament to that. As I reflect on this experience, I see how God was working in my favor. Although I took a significant pay cut when I moved to St. Croix, I made a promise to God that I would continue to tithe on my previous salary, and I did. I had faith that God would restore my salary, and by His grace, He did. What a blessing!

Today, I am happy to say my health has been restored. I have learned to do better managing how stress affects me. I practiced yoga, exercised at least five days a week, and continued to eat healthy. My blood pressure went from the stroke zone of 195/110 to numbers so low my doctor reduced my medication from 100mg of medication per day to 25mg. I now monitor my blood pressure daily, and my readings are normal or low (115/75). Ultimately, my goal is to be medication-free, and with God's help, I see that in my near future.

I'm not sure what my life would have been like had I not walked away from that situation. If my story can help one woman restore her health, the experience I went through will not have been in vain. **You may not need to quit your job**, but I am urging you ladies to take charge of your health. Monitor your blood pressure, try introducing healthy options in your diet, and find ways to reduce and manage your stress. Your health is your wealth – protect it!

Let's do our part to reverse these unbelievable statistics **where one woman dies every minute of heart disease**. If we all step up and do something each day to address this issue, I truly believe that we can get to the heart of the matter.

Loving Life Anew

By Diann Antley

Oftentimes, you'll hear of how little girls are so in tuned to their fathers, they inherit the label 'Daddy's Little Girl.' Even the writing of television sitcoms and bestsellers depict such love and affection. While the ending of a great show or book would have you believe the role model of the family was the "girl's first love," mine was actually my first heartbreak. We butt heads and clashed in personalities for as long as I could remember. Nothing I said or did appeared to be good enough. It was challenging enough growing up shy, awkward and introverted. Adding the lack of affection and attention from my father made things worse. Little did I know that our dysfunctional relationship would put me on a journey of carrying emotional wounds while taking detours which led to some bad life decisions.

I'm reminded of a time when my parents saw me outside having a casual conversation with a young man. It was no big deal to me; however, my father seemed to have thought otherwise. I could see on his face that he wasn't pleased, so I ended the conversation and returned home. I was sitting on the sofa and speaking to one of our relatives on the phone when my parents returned from the grocery store. My dad pointed at me and said, "See? I don't care about her...". Why would any parent say such a thing about their own child? He probably didn't think I heard him, but I did. That was just one of many unpleasant remarks I would hear him make about me. For the longest time, I could not understand why my dad had a negative attitude towards me. It was hurtful and there's only so much a person can take before exploding...

One morning, I found myself rushing out of the house to catch the bus I needed to successfully transfer to the train and arrive to work on time. I remember my dad wanted to walk out with me, but I hurried out and didn't hold the door. He became very upset with me. The next thing I knew, we were arguing while walking to the bus stop. It was crazy, but it was also long overdue. All my bottled-up emotions came out during that argument. I felt horrible about how I exploded. As soon as I reached work, I contacted my mama to let her know what happened. She merely stated that we would discuss it when we arrived home that evening.

During our discussion, I found out why there had been years of negativity directed towards me. Apparently, I reminded my dad of his mother, and the two of them NEVER got along. Their relationship was so strained that my dad dropped out of high school to join the Army just to get away from her. I honestly can't imagine a parent/child relationship being so bad the child would go through great lengths to escape from them. Knowing this pushed me closer to my mama because I didn't think I could talk to my dad about anything. It would have been nice if my father took the time to teach me about relationships, but I guess he couldn't if we barely had one of our own. Although I had two parents in my household, it felt as if I only had one. Therefore, I grew up looking for love and validation in all the wrong places and from all the wrong men.

I was searching for what I lacked as a child. I wanted what I felt my dad did not give me. I THOUGHT I found it...

While visiting relatives who were having a gathering at their home, I noticed a man I'd never seen before. He was quite attractive. I guess he thought the same about me because my cousin had to constantly tell him to stop looking at me, Lol. By the end of the evening, the gentleman shook my hand and proceeded to slip me his phone number. I waited a few days before contacting him. That first phone call resulted in our first date which led to daily phone calls and more dates. He was truly acting like a gentleman; indeed, a real prince charming.

We spent a lot of time together and I got accustomed to him taking me out for a drive. On one occasion, as I enjoyed his company, I didn't realize he had driven me out of NYC. I jokingly asked if I was being kidnapped and needed to call the police. We ended up in Pennsylvania. The scenery was so beautiful, and with its vibrant colors, it was breathtaking. Plus, dining out in PA was a treat to me.

There were many "what ifs" on this day trip. What if we spent quality time out here? What if we casually looked at houses? What if we inquired about owning property? Before you knew it, those "what ifs" became a reality. Almost magically, we got married, and I purchased a home in East Stroudsburg, PA.

I was satisfied. I thought I'd finally found someone who would love me the way I craved to be loved. I thought moving away and beginning a new life was what I needed, and the memories of my past wouldn't matter anymore. But I thought wrong. Six months after we moved into our new home and began getting used to our new lives together, while retiring for the evening, my husband told me that he would NOT be able to financially contribute to our household. Needless to say, I. Was. In. Shock.

The next morning, I woke up asking myself "how could this be happening"? We were both getting up every morning, getting dressed, driving to the bus stop and commuting into NYC. I KNEW he had a job because I had visited him at his place of employment on a few occasions. I also KNEW he did not have to pay child support because I celebrated with him as he received letters in the mail indicating the completion of payments. So, where was his money going? Better yet, why wasn't it going towards this house I thought we were turning into a home? Of course, I had more questions than answers.

As days turned into weeks and months, I became stressed and angry. I was solely responsible for paying the mortgage, utility bills, my student loans, our cell phone bills, keeping food on the table and everything else. My savings depleted rapidly. It didn't take long before I found myself in a major financial sinkhole. Every bill was behind in payments, including the mortgage. I made attempts to have the loan modified, but the bank I was dealing with only agreed to do so by LESS THAN $5.00. I was outraged. I had no idea how I was going to survive. Furthermore, I had to discontinue my online college courses.

This was not going to work. I was now tens of thousands of dollars in debt, with no visible way out. To make matters worse, my husband became ill and needed surgery. It would take weeks for him to make a full recovery, but he decided to use this as an opportunity to retire early. It wasn't that he couldn't work anymore.

He chose not to and made the decision without discussing it with me. Not only was I the only one contributing to the household, I became the only one employed. With little options, I filed for bankruptcy thinking that would help. It didn't.

Our marriage became two people who resided in the same place but didn't sleep together or speak to each other. I was miserable. I had looked for love in the wrong man and found myself broke, broken and hurt. I wanted out, but that wasn't the Christian thing to do, was it? I had plenty of sleepless nights contemplating if God would be upset with me because I didn't want to stay in my marriage. I asked Him to forgive me and I separated from my husband. After failed attempts to get financial assistance elsewhere and to have a short sale performed on the property, I painfully walked away from my house. I felt like a failure. As a wife. As a homeowner. As a human being.

In January 2015, I woke up and found myself divorced, bankrupt and about to lose my home forever. This was a very humiliating experience for me because I waited so long to get married, trying to avoid the exact situations I endured. I thought, "If I were older and he was older than me, my life would be different from other marriages because I wouldn't have to go through the nonsense and foolery." Instead, everything that was being built fell apart around me. The only thing left for me to do was to find a way to mend the broken pieces of my existence. Not because I wanted to, but because I had to. I'd fallen on my back from every situation I was in. The only way to begin to repair the pieces of my life was to surrender. Forgive and let it all go. At this point, it was time to LIFT myself out of brokenness and LAUNCH forward in my process towards LEADING into ANEW person.

I wanted God to do a new thing in me. But before He could do it, I had to close this part of my life. This was a pivotal moment because God needed me to understand the importance of forgiveness. You see, no matter what it is we are going through, we have choices in how we react. One Sunday, after church, while sitting in my vehicle at the church's parking lot, the Holy Spirit instructed me to call my ex-husband and apologize for the role I played in everything. When I called him and told him that I forgave him for what happened between us and asked for forgiveness in how I responded, he accepted my apology. It was time to forgive and let it all go. Indeed, God couldn't bless my future if I was holding on to things of my past that no longer serve me.

Now that I had finally let it all go, there was room for God to maneuver. He was there all along, but sometimes God will sit quietly while you grow through your circumstances because teachers are often quiet during tests. I had no idea how I was going to pay my current bills and catch up on the late ones, but I knew it would happen. Faithfully, God provided all that I needed. He had me downsize from a three-bedroom, two and one-half bathroom house to a two-bedroom apartment. I took what was absolutely necessary and left the rest behind. This was a new season to start over.

Even though I had my full-time job, I required another stream of income in order to tackle my expenses better, since the money I was making wasn't enough to get me back on track. That's when I was blessed with the opportunity to become an entrepreneur. A woman from my church approached me and asked if I wanted to attend a function at her home. I accepted the invitation and went. Unbeknown to me, that function led me to starting my own travel business. It was a major leap and I had a lot to learn since I never owned a business before. Still, I felt this was exactly what I needed to turn my life around.

Initially, I named my business after the family (Antley's Travel), but I believed God had other plans when the name was changed to Anew You Travel. I had no idea back then that name would mean so much to me today. I KNEW God was at work, providing something that helped save me financially and naming it as a reminder of how He saved me spiritually. Now, I am running my travel business full-time and it is thriving, having won the Pocono Records 2018 Readers' Choice Award for Best Travel Agency. To God Be The Glory!

As time passed, I found myself sorting out the things that happened in my childhood and my marriage. I learned to separate myself from the negatives, worked on my mind, soul and spirit, and sought those attributes that would help me regain my passion for life. I THOUGHT I needed someone else to love me and to build a life together, but I found out I wasn't ready. I needed to heal emotionally from my childhood wounds. I needed to love myself more and strengthen my relationship with God. While I still believe in the constitution of marriage, I know that whomever God has for me is for me. I need only to get out of the way and allow Him to work. God also reminded me that I must be willing to grow through the process of healing. Simply put, I was slowly but surely living my life anew.

Won't God LIFT, Lead and Launch you? Yes, He will! Today, I stand no longer broke and broken but repaired and anew. You can't make this stuff up! I'm someone who wants you to know if I can do it, so can you. It won't be easy, but nothing worth it ever is.

By sharing my story, my hope and prayer is it has helped you understand there are others who have gone through negative life events, but the key to all of this is to GROW THROUGH. You don't have to stay in a marriage that you shouldn't be in. You don't have to struggle financially for the rest of your life. When one door closes, God is sure to open a better one. Be encouraged and "know that all things work together for good to them that love God, to them who are the called according to his purpose" (Romans 8:28 KJV).

As I continue to walk in forgiveness, love and abundance, I encourage you to find your path and do the same. Remember, God makes ALL things new.

Here's to anew You!

"Nor is new wine put into old wineskins [that have lost their elasticity]; otherwise the wineskins burst, and the [fermenting] wine spills and the wineskins are ruined. But new wine is put into fresh wineskins, so both are preserved" (Matthew 9:17 AMP).

Bruised But Not Broken

By Rev. T'Shawn Rivers

"You, Lord, took up my case; You redeemed my life." ~
Lamentations 3:58

Raised in Brooklyn, New York, I had a wonderful childhood. I had a blessed but sheltered upbringing and felt like I could tackle anything. When I reached my teenage years, I had a little more freedom to explore the things my parents were protecting me from. I started to grow up and act out. Little did I know, I was on my way to the school of hard knocks and the lessons were going to be harder than any academic test I'd ever taken. These lessons caused a lot of hurt and pain, leaving me bruised but not broken. Why? Because God has a plan for my life. He did not want me to be defeated.

After graduating from the Philippa Schuyler Middle School for the Gifted and Talented, I passed an entrance exam and was accepted into the Erasmus Hall High School of Performing Arts. Throughout my academic years, I strived to be more, do more, and learn more. The academic competition was fierce, trying to maintain high grades and compete against so many students. I was breaking the "glass ceiling" in the education system as a young girl of color. My life in high school was incredibly exciting and I loved every minute of it.

It felt like I was on a fast track. Everything was starting to speed up in my life. I found myself staying out late at parties and meeting different people who were involved in all kinds of behaviors like underage drinking. The more I hung around this new crowd, the more I ignored my responsibilities at school and at home. I even started to sample alcohol. My parents had no idea; I hid the truth about my tardiness and slipping grades by telling them that I had taken on too many commitments, promising to do better. Since I was still active in church, my parents weren't so concerned.

My good girl image was convincing; then I met my high school crush who swept me off my feet. I was so in love with him and he was in love with me; we were inseparable. Thinking he would be my soulmate forever, I rapidly went from good girl to bad. By age sixteen, I was cutting school and following my love interest everywhere, even to places I knew no self-respecting girl should be.

This was the beginning of a downward spiral of bad adolescent decisions and grown up mistakes that a young girl couldn't afford to make. My boyfriend started hanging out with the wrong crowd, exploring his interest in music and striving to make it in the entertainment industry. His friends were into drugs and other seedy behavior, but he thought he could handle it and I wanted to be with him no matter what, until drugs entered the picture. Oh boy! This was not something I wanted to do, nor was it something I wanted him to do. He, however, wouldn't listen to me, so I cautiously tagged along.

My soulmate was changing. He was always looking for ways to get money so that he could get high. I was afraid and annoyed. I told him that drugs were a bad idea, but he needed to "fit in." Things were getting worse; he dropped out of school and became obsessed and possessive. What happened to my friend, the love of my life? What was going to happen to us? I had to do something. Surely, he would understand where I was coming from. The least I could do was try to fix this.

Then, it happened. No one had ever hit me like that before. One moment I was talking to him about his drug use and so-called friends and the next minute I was on the floor, holding the right side of my face. My best friend had struck me without warning! I was devastated, sobbing in disbelief. What had I done to cause this? And how could I make things right? I didn't know what to do; all I knew is that I was confused, hurt and afraid. Ironically, I was blaming myself and didn't know why.

My boyfriend let's call him "Ben," as in "been there, done that," helped me up, held me in his arms and apologized profusely. He said he had not slept much the night before and had a lot on his mind. I accepted his apology and we continued our relationship as if nothing had ever happened. This was a freak incident, no harm, no foul. I had nothing more to worry about and we would get through this together. One could only hope. Ben stayed drug-free and tried to improve his behavior as we got back to normal, so-to-speak. I was spending more time at school to prepare for mid-terms, and he was still trying to pursue his music career. Things seemed to be stable, but it didn't last.

One afternoon, my girlfriend and I decided to go to a popular game room where a lot of our friends would hang out after school to play games, pool and listen to music. The usual gang was there, including Ben and some of his "friends" who had gotten him into drugs in the past. He saw me and looked surprised and then annoyed, which both worried and angered me, but I kept my cool. I gave him a kiss on the cheek and asked him how his day went. He shrugged and said it was fine and that he would catch up with me later. Acknowledging the brush off and realizing he was high, I left. He said, "You should go home. I'll call you later." I said nothing and left.

Feeling dejected, my girlfriend and I went to her house to hang out. She tried to cheer me up with the "boys will be boys" talk, but I was still feeling like something was off. You know that "women's intuition" that fuels your curiosity and concern that "something in the milk ain't clean?" The feeling that indicates things are about to get worse? That's what I was feeling, and it was strong. We continued to talk about this and that, did each other's makeup, and had a fun afternoon. I was glad I had an opportunity to be with my friend and do girl stuff.

On my way home from her house, as she was walking me part of the way, we saw Ben and his friend walking towards us. Once he saw me, he appeared irritated. My friend and I looked at each other, then I asked, "What's wrong with Ben?" She said, "Maybe he's angry that you are with me and not at home." Whatever the case, I tried to be upbeat and positive and put a smile on my face. Immediately, when Ben and I approached each other, he put his arm around me and pulled me aside.

He was indeed angry that I had not gone straight home but even angrier when he noticed I had makeup on. We debated and argued a bit. I tried to keep our dispute contained, but it was obvious that he was high, and his anger was spiking. At that point, I knew it would be best for me to go home and not say anything more. When I turned to walk away, Ben grabbed me from behind, spun me around and slapped me across the face in the middle of the street. He held me by my collar and shook me violently, cursing and yelling.

I struggled to break free and defend myself, but it was useless; he was much stronger than me. Both of our friends grabbed him and told him to stop, but he was not in his right mind; he was in a rage. People also yelled and cursed at him, saying they called the police, which helped me as he turned his attention to them. Finally, I got free with my jacket torn and ran home.

I cried and wondered how I let myself get into such a tragic situation. It was late evening when I arrived home. Still, my mother was up waiting for me, worried about her youngest daughter. I kissed her on the cheek and apologized for getting home late. She noticed the bruises on my face and my torn jacket, and then asked what happened. I lied and said I had a fight with a girl and not to worry, I was fine. I prayed for God to open my eyes and help me, then went to bed, crying myself to sleep.

I went to school the next day, bruises and all. I did not see Ben and I didn't want to see him. I was heartbroken, but I was done. I loved Ben, but I came to the conclusion that he loved drugs more and had become someone else. The Ben I knew and loved was gone. Weeks passed before I saw him again. He called my house every night. My mom or dad would tell him I was not available or did not want to talk. Ben even had friends call and ask for me so that he could get my attention. I would simply hang up, I was done—so I thought.

After weeks of ignoring Ben, he showed up one day after school with flowers. I hesitated, but he assured me that he would not hurt me and only wanted a chance to explain. So, after hours of walking and talking, we were together again, just like that. Why? Because I truly did love him, but things didn't stay calm for Ben and me. We continued to have a tumultuous relationship after a month of reconciling. I also became a teenage mom and moved out of my parents' home shortly before my eighteenth birthday. Then, a few months later, Ben and I were married. This was heartbreaking for my parents, so I was determined to prove to them that becoming a mother at an early age would not interfere with my future as a successful woman.

Although my parents were heartbroken, they allowed me to move on and make my own decisions. With my baby and packed belongings, I moved out to live with Ben's sister then moved in with my sister until I could find my own place. It was a very stressful first couple of months as a teen mom, living from pillar to post. Ben was struggling to keep employment and I was trying to find a program that would let me finish out my last year of high school with my baby in tow. I was feeling defeated and I missed life the way it used to be, but I had a little life to care for now.

Feeling the stress of fatherhood and not being able to keep a job, Ben relapsed into drugs, this time "graduating" from cocaine to crack. He would steal anything that wasn't nailed down to feed his habit, and I knew my baby and I were in trouble. I was fortunate enough to find a job, but I was struggling because I couldn't keep money on me, and I couldn't keep anything of value in the house. There were times I had to sleep with my baby close and a knife under my pillow because I never knew what state of mind Ben would be in when he eventually decided to show up. There were many sleepless nights, sometimes fighting until the wee hours of the morning. Then, after being rushed to the hospital with a ruptured eardrum after Ben had struck me with full force, I'd had enough.

I had to escape this tortured relationship once and for all! So, I prayed to God with all that I had, and finally got the courage to leave for good. I confided in my sister about the abuse, and she took me and my baby in. On the basis of domestic violence, I pulled all documents together to start divorce proceedings. It was a very painful, emotional ordeal, and at times dangerous. Ben's mind had been altered so much from the drugs that he saw me as his property and his meal ticket to drugs. I was no longer his wife or soulmate. Our fairytale romance was over.

After months of family and criminal court proceedings, a judge ruled in my favor and granted me full custody with a divorce. I cried emotional tears of relief and dismay. I was free, I was blessed, I was alive, and now it was me and my child against the world. I persevered and overcame one of the most difficult chapters in my young life. It was a tough next couple of years after the divorce and the entire domestic violence ordeal.

Both my child and I struggled with post-traumatic stress disorder symptoms, often having flashbacks and nightmares about some of the most heated physical fights. It took a lot of prayers, meditation, and faith to come through those trying times. I had a little life to make a difference for, and that was my primary reason for living and fighting so very hard. I had a chance at a new beginning. I was delivered from the bondage of abuse that imprisoned me for too long. Finally, I was liberated.

I never thought I would have endured domestic violence. The pain from being abused physically, emotionally and spiritually was shocking and demeaning. There was no hope that I could see; yet by keeping the faith in God and being strong and persistent, I was able to break the chains of bondage that kept me pinned down. This is my testimony, that after surviving one of the most painful experiences in my life, I am grateful to be here to fulfill God's plan for my life. Indeed, I was bruised, but I am not broken.

If ever you find yourself in what seems like an impossible, negative situation, know that you are not alone. You can overcome any obstacle that is placed in your path. You are strong and you are blessed! God has a plan for you to live your best life. You have the power to persevere and break the chains of bondage.

"I can do all things through Christ who strengthens me."
~ Philippians 4:13

Trust God and Faith It

By N. Lynne Henderson

There will come a time in your life that you will have to trust God even when you don't see Him anywhere in sight. Did you ever think that the path of your life would be a simple one, without curves, dips or dead ends? Life is hard but full of experiences that will teach us if we are willing to learn. Even if we are not willing to learn, life's lessons will still find their way to us, giving us the opportunity to learn how to trust God.

I've always been independent and worked hard to obtain what I needed, so when it came to trusting God in the area of my finances, I never really did. My jobs paid well which made it easy to buy whatever I wanted. I was single, financially stable and taking care of myself. But one day, it all changed. The Lord had a plan to show me how to trust Him for everything. It wasn't easy for me, but I had to learn how to lean completely on God.

For many years, I had been working in corporate America when a mass layoff was announced. We were told the layoffs would happen in phases. My day came, and I was called into the office and given a "last day" date. Although we had been given the date previously, it didn't matter. I was scared. I had never been laid off a job before. What was I going to do now? Thankfully, I received a severance package and was able to pursue a life-long passion of going to culinary school.

After completing my culinary courses, I started a family business. It was growing; things were moving along when one of my partners unexpectedly walked out of the business, not even at the end of the day; no two weeks' notice, nothing. They just decided they didn't want to do this journey with us anymore. I was shocked and angry. We had signed a five-year lease with no exit strategy in place. By faith, we had launched out on a dream and now our faith was being shaken. Our business was on the verge of crumbling right before our eyes. What were we going to do now? God was showing me again, that my trust in Him had to be solid through every season in my life, and through every business venture. We stayed open a few more years and eventually closed.

For a while, this experience left me discouraged with a bad taste in my mouth for business. I had exercised faith, trusted, and still failed. Our dream business was gone, never to return. What was I going to do now? I had been out of corporate America for over ten years. Who would hire me? What kind of skills would I need to get back in the game? There were a lot of uncertainties about my next job, but I was able to secure a position and was happy about the new opportunities that awaited me. I adjusted myself to the workforce again, and then suddenly—two years in—I got called into the office and was fired. Yes, that's right, fired! I got kicked out of a job again. I was crushed. Laid off the first time, fired this time. I was angry, disappointed, and hurt. What was happening? This second "job loss" experience was embarrassing, but it lit a fire inside of me to continue pursuing entrepreneurship.

Working for others did not give me the chance to experience the success I wanted. All I had to show for it were long hours, no recognition, extra responsibilities, and a pink slip. Indeed, my faith in the Lord continued to be tried. God was doing His work and it was working. I was more determined than ever to operate a business for myself; I refused to give up on all my hopes and dreams, so I launched out into another enterprise. There was nothing to lose at this point. My faith was growing, and I didn't intend to look back.

Inspired by a message at church one Sunday in July 2016, I came home and started making plans to move. Although I wasn't working at the time, my faith was. I was learning to trust God at a new level and to really walk by faith. Learning to do it afraid, I stepped out on my dreams with the Lord in front of me, guiding me all the way. A week later, I had keys to my new apartment, then a few months afterward, I started an E-Commerce business venturing out into new territory. This type of business always interested me, but I didn't know much about it, so I was extremely grateful that everyone and everything I needed for this new journey was placed strategically in my path. Implementing while learning, I made strides and decided to leap all the way in and became fully self-employed in January 2018.

That decision didn't stop the challenges. This new journey of *total trust and faith* was teaching me to finally live what I believed and told others all the time. "Trust God" even when your rent and light bill are due. My faith was steadily increasing. I was learning to (F) fix my eyes, (A) accept His grace, (I) invite His perspective, (T) train my lips, and (H) hide in His presence. (I) It was an individual (T) test. All my life's circumstances were teaching me this. It was hard and grueling, but peaceful and rewarding at the same time. The God that I knew and served always came through, every time, every single time.

Furthermore, when I looked over my life, I knew I was born to be an entrepreneur. They say that being motivated by challenges is one of the signs and characteristics that you were born to be an entrepreneur. Well, trials constantly motivate me. One such situation was the time I failed out of college while pursuing a degree in engineering. This was a hard lesson in failure, but I refused to quit. After transferring, going to summer school, and bringing up my grades, I was able to graduate with a dual degree. This experience taught me perseverance. Perseverance has become one of my favorite words and I've learned to persevere through every season, good and bad.

Throughout my life, I have been able to overcome barriers, tough times, and even lean times. Every one of my dreams to succeed has been tested. In spite of it all, I have faced my failures and remained full of faith through the challenges. My shoulders are squared, and I have reminded myself that I was born for this—born to conquer, born to succeed, and born to be great. Incidentally, I'm amused when I think about the statement "I was born for this" because I was born literally fighting for my life.

As an infant, at six months, I had to have hernia surgery that left me with an incision the length of my entire body. God showed me that He was teaching me way back then how to be a fighter, how to be more than a conqueror. He is still teaching me today to overcome obstacles that try to prevent me from living my best life. As a result of the scar from my surgery, I never wore two-piece swimwear, but it didn't stop me from swimming. I made the necessary adjustments and accomplished the task knowing I must adjust to life's circumstances and move on. This is something I learned very early in life.

I've also learned to live free in my journey. Free from every and anything that prevents me from fulfilling God's purpose for my life and business. I refuse to put my dreams on the shelf anymore. As a matter of fact, I know that if I follow God's map for my life and not my own, I will succeed. He made the map, so He knows the journey, and everything involved in it. Although the journey will have dips, hills, puddles, valleys, and mountains, I won't end up stuck. There were emotional valleys, valleys of sickness and loss along with numerous financial valleys that found their way to my door. One time, I had no health insurance and needed major surgery. My only choice was to apply for Charity Care, which was one of the most humiliating experiences of my life, but I survived it. Despite my valleys, God has always led me out of every single one and provided everything I needed. He has never failed.

Recently, another financial hurdle came my way. An extension for my tax filing was processed by my accountant. When the appointment came, I was told that a balance of $27,000 was owed. Sitting across from his desk, horrified, I stopped myself from bursting into tears. Burdened down and stressed out, I left his office. The next two days, I felt myself going down into a hole of despair. My mind was overwhelmed, and it was hard to digest this information. All kinds of thoughts crossed my mind. I didn't have this kind of money; how would I be able to pay it back? I didn't want to go to jail. Prayer and gratitude kept me from going into a deep depression.

As the accountant and I had agreed, the numbers were recalculated and resent. Sure enough, there had been a calculation error. The next day I received an email saying I owed less than ten percent of the original number quoted. "Thank You, Jesus" echoed all through my being. The Lord had shown me again that when I trust Him, He will work everything out. My faith and trust in God had to be literally excavated. There was no one else to go to; He was my only option. After crying out, He brought me out again and I constantly remind myself of His faithfulness, His love, and His provisions for me.

I encourage you to do the same. Let your faith and trust in God take root so much so that you won't waver, no matter what. Remind yourself of His exploits, how He always provides, always makes a way, always looks out for you. Always. If you are in business, or plan on going into business, know that you will have roadblocks and challenges that will discourage you. Thoughts will come to your mind to throw the whole thing in the garbage. Don't! Your faith is being challenged to indeed believe the vision that you were given. That idea was birthed from God. You're supposed to launch that idea. No success comes without hard times or circumstances.

Sometimes singles may feel that their success is tied to having a life partner. It's not. You can be single and successful. God is with you. You don't have to be married to be successful or to be financially stable. You are enough. Yes, you, yourself and you. With the Lord on your side, there is nothing that you can't accomplish. Let trust and faith lead your path in this journey of entrepreneurship. When you have God, He will make sure that you have everything you need. Pray, a lot; read your Bible and declare what He says about you and your business. You won't go wrong following His lead. I promise you, His Word is true and if you believe Him, follow His roadmap, and do what He says, you and your business will be successful.

If you've lost trust, trust again. If you've lost faith, have faith again. Dare to jump out and dream again. Write down your vision, pray over it, plan it out. You can do it. Let God be your source. Don't depend on others to be what God wants to be in your life. Don't let anyone be a space holder in your life for anything, whatever it might be, emotional support, financial support, or otherwise. Only God holds the key to your success. He also has the roadmap. He will interrupt your scheduled plan of events and show you His plan for you.

Again, I encourage you to "trust in the Lord with all your heart and lean not unto your own understanding... and He will direct your path" (Proverbs 3:5, 6b). Step out on **FAITH** and do **IT** again.

- **Fix** your eyes on Him. Let Him lead you; focus.
- **Accept** His grace. He has empowered you with all you need to get the job done; He is with you in this journey.
- **Invite** His perspective. He has the plan and He knows it better than you ever could. If you invite Him, He will indeed show you. Submerge your business in prayer. Don't do any business forecasting, business deals, or transactions without it.
- **Tame** your tongue. Teach and train your lips not to curse your life or business. Life and death are in the power of the tongue (Proverbs 18:21). Whatever you say, you can have. Declare His thoughts over your life and your business. Finally,

- **Hide** in His presence. Practice a life in His presence through prayer, His Word, and worship. When you hide in His presence, nothing can touch, harm, or destroy you! Psalm 91:4 says that He will cover you under His wings.
- **Individual**. This is an individual walk between you and God. It's individual, but you're not alone.
- **Test**. It's a test! A test that you can pass. Don't be afraid to try again, even if you've failed before. Pursue your dreams, *Trust God*, *Faith It*, and you'll succeed.

Soar to Your Destiny

By Rosie Thames

Life is a journey we all travel, and along that journey, there may be obstacles, setbacks and some turbulent moments—moments where you question your existence and question if you will ever make it to your God-intended destination. People often say, "God won't give you more than you can bear." Really, says who? I know they mean well, but I honestly wish people would stop throwing that phrase around especially during times when I feel like I am literally going through hell!

Question: have you ever felt like you were on the devil's hit list? Like all hell is unleashed against you, and it seems as if out of the billions of people on this planet the only persons of interest are you and your loved ones. The enemy won't give you a second to catch your breath. From one attack to the next, they send one storm after the other and their ultimate goal is to destroy your life. And in the midst of that you ask, "God, where on earth are You... don't You see I need HELP?!"

For three years, I've been desperately seeking God for a miracle. In the summer of 2014, my husband was diagnosed with lupus, a disease that attacked his kidneys causing renal failure. We had just returned from a three-year overseas assignment in Japan and was in the process of settling at our new duty assignment here in the United States. Things were challenging prior to our move causing a lot of tension in our marriage and the stressors of moving intensified it even more. We had two children, and both of us had been serving in the military for 13 years.

Despite all that was going on with my husband's health and losing his military career because of it, we were achieving much success in the business we started a few years back. We were growing a massive team, earning six figures in our 30s and were recognized as top income earners, reaching the highest level in our company. We were that "Power Couple" featured in the popular business magazine "Success from Home," featured in our company's success videos and sought-after speakers at local and national events because of our many achievements. Still, all this success did not prevent the storms of life from happening.

There was a season when I had had enough of it...LIFE! It was just cruel. I couldn't understand why all these things were happening to me. Each year, the attacks seemed more and more intense like a vicious cycle. They were way too much to handle.

A year after we had relocated and settled at our new duty assignment in the United States, things got bad in our marriage, and my husband was looking for a way out. We got so busy being successful, being parents, in addition to many other responsibilities that we grew away from each other. We were devoted to enriching other families' lives while our family was falling apart. Moreover, my husband blamed me for his illness because of something I said to him out of anger in the past. I begged for his forgiveness, but obviously he was still holding on to it. I was devastated, I was broken, and I got bitter. How did we get here? Our marriage wasn't that bad, or so I thought. It was apparent I was no longer the woman he desired. He said I was a nagging wife and way too sensitive, and frankly, he was not the man I fell in love with 12 years ago. He was insensitive, unaffectionate, and he barely talked to me plus he started to avoid me by devoting most of his time on the business.

While I was healing from the pain of his rejection, my mom fell severely ill during her visit for Thanksgiving. She had been battling with cancer for years. She had a mastectomy and went through chemotherapy years ago, and the cancer was under remission. Still, I knew when she came to visit that she wasn't well, but I didn't know she wasn't going to make it back home. My mom fell gravely ill on my birthday, November 26, 2016. I rushed her to the emergency room where they delivered the horrible news that her intestines had collapsed and on top of that she had stage 4 cancer which had spread to her lungs, liver, and bones. Her prognosis was not looking good, but I didn't want to accept that because I believe God is a healer and believed He was going to heal my mother along with my husband.

During the weeks she was in the hospital, I prayed and fasted yet each time I saw her she grew weaker. The doctor gave her a few weeks to live, but I refused to believe him. My God is Jehovah-Rapha, the God who heals. Upon her discharge, she came home with me while on hospice care and died a few weeks later. I was crushed! Why would God allow this? I did everything I knew to do; I prayed and fasted believing He would heal her. My faith was under attack because I just couldn't understand why? She was only 57 years old, and I wasn't ready for her to go.

I loved my mom dearly, but there were issues we didn't get to resolve from my childhood that I was still dealing with. Growing up, I was afraid of my mom and to this day, I sometimes have nightmares as an adult from moments of my childhood; she was harder on me than any of my other siblings. But it doesn't matter now. I understood why and I wanted her to know that. I desperately wanted that mother/daughter relationship I lacked growing up, and now that opportunity is gone.

What do you do when God's plan isn't lining up with the plans you have for your life? Plus, where do you turn when the direction, He is taking you seems to be totally off course? God's plan doesn't make sense most of the time, and we don't always get what we pray for. So, what do you do in those moments? I've learned the best thing to do is just keep trusting. But I must be honest, trusting God can be quite challenging since things will not be perfect and you often won't see the full picture. However, even when you can't see what God is doing, when the visibility is low, you can trust Him to navigate you above the clouds through those dark moments. These are the times when I truly must apply what I have believed all my life. I have to trust God even when He says no.

In that same year when I lost my mom, we lost three other relatives, and I was just over it at that moment. It seemed like our prayers were going unanswered and there were days when I wondered why bother, why pray for healing because obviously God had other plans in mind. Nevertheless, my husband and I were still pressing towards our goals and that year we were recognized for reaching the top level in our company as Double Platinum Presidential Directors. I knew God's hands were still on our lives, and

He was still prospering us in other ways despite the trials.

I've heard that life is a series of storms. You are either in a storm, coming out of a storm or heading into a storm. In this life, you will face some storms. It's not a matter of if but when they will occur. In fact, if you are on this journey long enough, you are bound to face multiple storms. Well, I only wished someone had predicted 2018 because that year was packed with storms, the mother of all storms, a Category 5 catastrophic storm—the Katrina of all storms!

Let me tell you, the devil unleashed it all and he had no remorse! While still dealing with grief, my husband received the news that his father passed away. This was February 22, 2018, the very day my husband celebrated his 38th birthday. His dad was battling lung cancer for some time and later succumbed to pneumonia. Approximately two months later, my six-year-old son was admitted to the pediatric intensive care unit (PICU) for two weeks in critical condition. His right lung had collapsed due to pneumonia caused by strep. At that time, I also was seven months pregnant with our third child. Fear was consuming me; I didn't know what to do. My heart was beyond overwhelmed; this was more than I could bear.

I was spending so much time at the hospital with my son that I started to have early contractions. I wasn't sleeping, eating or taking care of myself well enough because all I could think about was my child who was severely ill. By the grace of God, he survived that storm, but as we were celebrating that victory, catching our breath from the ordeal, and preparing for the birth of our newborn in the coming month, my husband was now admitted in the hospital. His blood pressure was dangerously high, and the medical team was trying everything they could do to regulate it. The problem was that his blood pressure affected his kidney function so at this point he was at the end stage of renal failure at a 5 GFR rate! Now here we were fighting for my husband's life and eight months pregnant.

The doctors told him he would have to be on dialysis and recommended a kidney transplant. I just couldn't understand why me, why my family and why we had to endure all this. "Is there a purpose for this storm?" "Is this what life was meant to be?" "Is this why You created me?" "There has to be more to life than this?!" Yes, those were a series of questions I asked God when I was at the end of my rope, ready to throw in the towel on everything.

At this point, my mind was in such confusion, and I was overcome with intense fear, anxiety, and sadness. Am I going to lose my husband? This can't be. *This is way too much to handle, God.* I CAN'T do this anymore! After a moment of screaming and crying out loud, I came to my senses and realized I had a choice to make. Regardless of the reality of my situation, I can either choose God or choose to walk away from my faith in Him. I can either choose to live in fear or choose His peace.

Without hesitation, I boldly made a choice. I declared out loud for the enemy and all to hear "God is all I know, I know of nothing else and though He slays me yet will I trust Him!" Even though I didn't know who was responsible for the storms, I chose to face them with God on my side. Whether God had allowed these storms, or it was solely the plans of the enemy to wage war against my life, it didn't matter because I was confident that God would never fail me, and He would fight my battles for me.

At this very moment, as I am writing this chapter, my husband is connected to his dialysis machine that he does every night for nine hours and is currently on a kidney transplant list. Nevertheless, I am still praying and believing for supernatural healing from God whichever way He chooses to do it. I still choose to believe and trust God no matter what comes my way, and I know that God didn't bring us this far to abandon us. I am certain He is on this journey with us and He who started a good work in us will bring it to completion.

It's been said that what doesn't kill you makes you stronger, and I agree with that statement one hundred percent. Though at times I wished we had never encountered these storms, we have learned so many valuable lessons as a family. We have seen the power of restoration in our marriage through much prayer, counseling, and mentorship. God has worked tremendously in my husband and me. By His Spirit, He has taught us how to love unconditionally and to make our relationship a priority. We learned to devote more time to our marriage and our children and to value each other despite our shortcomings and flaws. Today we have helped many marriages and families overcome the very challenges we have faced so they too can thrive in their relationships.

I have learned so much throughout these experiences, and I am here to tell you there is a purpose for every storm that comes in your life. Each time you survive your storm, you become stronger, more resilient and deeper rooted. Will God put more on you than you can handle? Absolutely not! Yet, I believe with every storm, it is not my strength, but it is His strength that is made perfect in my weakness. Surely, I may not be able to handle the situation alone lest I boast in my own abilities but in learning to depend on God and in His might, I will have the strength to face and endure the storms of life because "I can do all things through Christ who strengthens me" (Philippians 4:13).

I no longer question God about the things I have endured throughout my life, because I now realize He has been writing and perfecting my story this entire time to share with the world. God has ministry for me to do and lives to impact. I am here on a mission and a divine assignment and come what may, despite all the darts, the attacks, the storms, the test and trials being launched by the enemy, I am learning more and more not to let them derail me or block me from my destiny. I must get back up, I must overcome, and I must fulfill the purpose God has for my life.

Webster's dictionary definition of soar is to rise high, maintaining height in air without using energy or power. It also defines destiny as a place intended to end or stop; a target, goal or purpose. We are all on a journey, a God intended destination and there is no way you can soar unless you get up off the ground, go through some clouds, face some storms and experience those turbulent moments. They are a part of our journey, and they are inevitable. You can't stay under it and you can't get around it, you must go through it and above it in order to have a better view of what's ahead so you can soar to your destiny and become the amazing person God created you to be.

Medication vs. Medicine:
God's Health Plan
By Darice Stephenson

"According as his divine power hath given unto us all things that pertain unto life and godliness, through the knowledge of him that hath called us to glory and virtue." ~ 2 Peter 1:3

Did you know most Americans are taking five or more prescription medications per day? Are you one of them? I certainly am no stranger to a life of medication dependency, yet God never intended for us to rely on medication to sustain our lives. Our Heavenly Father didn't just breathe life into us; He gave us everything pertaining to life and godliness. This includes natural remedies for when we find ourselves resisting sickness and disease. No matter the illness, God has given us power to overcome it and to live triumphantly in the area of health and wellness.

Although it may be a long journey, we are all capable of living victoriously without medication. I know; I endured many illnesses beginning at a very young age with motion sickness. By the age of 14, I was diagnosed with overactive thyroid disease (OATD) which required me to have my thyroid removed. That was my first surgery and prior to the procedure, I had to take seven different pills twice per day for 30 days. After the surgery, I was given another prescription with instructions to take that drug for the rest of my life to replace the hormone my thyroid was supposed to produce. Being a child, I had no choice at the time but to take the medication.

Years went by and living life without a thyroid wasn't bad; at least that is what I believed until I was diagnosed with lupus at age 30. Since I had never heard of this disease, my mind was overwhelmed with fear and confusing thoughts. I imagined the doctor was making it up until she handed me a pamphlet explaining that lupus was an autoimmune disease. I remember thinking to myself, "Am I going to die from this, or will I end up unable to live a normal life?" It seemed to me that my body would no longer function the way God created it to operate.

I prayed and cried out to God asking him to take this affliction away from me. God's response was *"For I know the thoughts that I think toward you, saith the Lord, thoughts of peace and not of evil, to give you an expected end" (Jeremiah. 29:11 KJV).* The fear of dying or becoming bedridden disappeared, but I still had to deal with the symptoms and being medicated. This reality made me earnestly seek God for answers regarding sickness and disease. Without a doubt, I knew it wasn't God's plan for me to live my life depending on medication.

Following the lupus diagnosis, I developed Raynaud's disease, which caused joint pains and much swelling in my knees. With every ailment, I had to depend on more medication, but the suffering did not end. At the age of 44, I experienced my first stroke followed by a series of seizures. These seizures were a result of my brain not getting enough oxygen while I slept, so I was placed on a sleep apnea machine. This stroke also left me with constant pain from nerve damage, blurred vision, and memory loss. Additionally, I suffered from chronic vertigo spells and severe coordination balance issues after a second episode occurred as stuttering strokes at age 49; the cause for this occurrence is still a mystery.

As if all that was not enough, I suffered from shingles not once but twice. Furthermore, because of fibroids, I have had a hysterectomy and have had more MRIs and blood draws than I can count. Despite all the drugs my doctors said were necessary for my treatment, I still was not getting better. In 2015, I was officially declared disabled. This bothered me because I knew the price was already paid for all sicknesses and diseases plaguing my life.

Being a born-again believer, I would remind myself that "We are fearfully and wonderfully made" (Psalms 139:14). I remembered also when I was diagnosed with lupus, my mother had given me a book titled, *Why Christians Get Sick* by Rev. George H. Malkmus. That book was the answer to my prayers, and it changed my life forever. It revealed to me God's health plan for man and taught me that my body was created to heal itself. After reading the book, I realized there are two parts to healing, spiritual and natural. Unfortunately, most believers focus more on the spiritual while ignoring the natural, which includes the body.

We have mastered the spiritual part of living by faith, knowing scripture and making declarations. However, the missing ingredient is how to care for our bodies naturally. I finally had the information I needed to regain my health and wellness. This was when I realized

I had to do the natural part by changing the way I ate. It was time to stop eating junk and start putting more nutrient-rich foods into my body. Although I did not know entirely what to do, I was determined to take responsibility for my health and be medication free.

At the beginning of my healing journey, I only ate salads with no dressing and drank carrot juice. Miraculously after three months, my doctors took me off the medications for lupus. Hallelujah! These results motivated me, so once I stopped taking all medication, I developed a passion to help others achieve the same. My life had a greater purpose and I became a Certified Health and Wellness Coach from the Institute of Integrative Nutrition in New York City. It was an exciting time. My company, Lifestyle Wellness Group, LLC was launched with me teaching and having workshops in my local church. The sacrifices to regain my health had paid off.

Life was going well without medications. I was a raw food chef teaching others how to take control of their health until the morning I woke up in a stroke and had to be rushed to the hospital. While in the emergency room, I had several seizures. This time I knew the cause of the illness. I was dealing with stress from being in a non-physical domestic violent marriage. The stroke caused nerve damaged, blurred vision and memory loss, but I had the use of my limbs. Once again, I was medication dependent.

I became very depressed, and anxiety attacks started to occur, which added to my symptoms. I asked God to give me the knowledge and wisdom that I was missing. Shortly after praying for an answer, several things began to happen. First, a friend of mine introduced me to essential oils. Next, an invitation came to learn about herbs and how to use them as medicine. A coincidence perhaps...or was God answering my prayers? I chose to believe He was answering and again I was on the road to restoring my health and well-being. At least so I thought.

I felt well enough to travel and continued to gain more knowledge and understanding. During my early battle with lupus, I remembered reading *Fasting Your Way to Health* by Lee Bueno-Aguer. This book had taught me that fasting was beneficial both spiritually and physically, so I decided to reread it. Thankfully, I did. It encouraged me to continue to seek answers through prayer and fasting.

In January 2018, I decided to go on an absolute fast for 40 days, which was a stretch for me. I had never fasted that long; the most extended fast for me was 21 days. During this 40 day fast, my focus was for total restoration; I wanted to experience living in perfect health. I prayed and asked God to give me the wisdom necessary to help myself and others. He took me to His word, in Jeremiah 30:17, and I was encouraged as I read, *"For I will restore health unto thee, and I will heal thee of thy wounds, saith the Lord..."*. I also recalled in the book *Fasting Your Way to Health*, the author talked about how fasting spiritually and naturally works hand in hand. Fasting allowed me to focus on my health and God's plans for my life.

I successfully completed the 40-day fast, but what I began to experience wasn't what I expected. I was having stuttering stroke symptoms that put me in the hospital for five days. After being released, I was on high doses of medication. I cried out to God, and I revisited everything I had learned both spiritually and naturally about the physical body. I realized I needed to flood my body with nutrients from the earth, for God has given us every herb and herb bearing seed for the healing of the body.

Let me be clear, I'm not against physicians or medication; I believe God gave us both physicians and medicine for a reason. If we look back in history, all medicine originated from the herbs of the earth. They came from plant-based ingredients, which God placed on the planet for the healing of our bodies. However, I am against long-term medication (pharmaceuticals). I understand that medication is necessary at times to sustain life, but they should be temporary. God didn't intend for His children to live life taking medication. The word medicine(s) is only mentioned four times in the Bible with three different meanings in the Old Testament. The word herb(s) appears thirty-seven times with eight different purposes. The significance is God has given us the information necessary for us to live on this earth.

Statistically, the average American takes at least five or more prescription drugs per day. Why? Truth is, we don't take time to gain the knowledge of how God created our bodies and the natural medicine (herbs) He has provided for us. In the scripture, Hosea 4:6 states, *"My people are destroyed for lack of knowledge..."* I believe there is an herb or plant for every sickness and disease including those not discovered. God didn't design our bodies to process chemicals. There is a common statement telling you to "let your food be your medicine," and there is some truth to it. If the food is rich in nutrients, it can be medicine. Unfortunately, we live in a world full of toxins, pesticides, and poisons and when these chemicals are in the soil, they eventually end up in our food source. Still, eating well is better than relying on medications to live well.

Once released from the hospital, I started flooding my body with herbs and superfruits and water. I discovered the trinity of health and wellness, which is detoxification, hydration, and nutrition. All three are necessary to obtain perfect health and to live as God intended for us to live. If we want to live in divine health, we must follow the original plan our Heavenly Father laid out for us. This is non-negotiable. What we put into our bodies will have a direct impact on our health.

Now that I've been able to regain control of my health and well-being, I am very passionate about assisting those who genuinely desire to reverse their health condition, so they too can live the abundant life God intended for them. One of my goals is to teach the clear distinction between medication and medicine. Medication is usually a prescribed drug by a healthcare professional. It is often chemically based, but natural supplements (medicines) are usually plant-based and can provide our bodies with the necessary nutrients. When we follow God's original health plan and utilize the spiritual (God's word) and natural (herbs) resources that He provided for His creation, we will be unstoppable to live a prosperous life in divine health.

Rising Above the Pain of Grief and Loss

By Cleo MeriAbut Jarvis

I had lost loved ones before, including two children, yet nothing prepared me for the pain I felt when I lost Mom. One minute we were playing around and the next, I was performing CPR on my closest friend, my mother. And, for a very brief moment, everything appeared to literally stand still. My vacation in paradise had turned into a nightmare. Mom had transitioned without any warning or time to say goodbye.

Like most westerners, I had been socialized to avoid dealing with death and loss at all costs. But I had been emotionally duped because *everyone* dies, and *loss is inevitable*! Since I was in a state of **loss-denial** and so deeply unprepared when the pain of loss came, it felt like a lightning bolt hit and shook the foundation of my part of the world. I later learned that the effects of the shock of loss are so significant that scientific researchers found the impact can be measured in the brain. They found that typically, a grieving person does a couple of things and I was no exception. I became numb, doing *almost nothing* for a while. I went to work like a zombie, merely "going through the motions." Functioning on emotional autopilot, I was physically and emotionally spent.

Next, I questioned everything. Who I was? Where I came from? And where I was going? I asked, "What is the point of doing all this crap if folks are going to drop dead like flies?" I was hurt and angry at the world. I screamed to the top of my lungs with my face stuffed in a pillow to muffle the sound. You see my mother's house was full of relatives, and I was especially concerned about my eight-year-old niece who lived with my mom from birth. It was a hard time for all of us, so I had to put my feelings aside because as the oldest, my family needed me. The level of stress was almost unbearable. I needed help and fast!

As I cried, I could feel Mom's presence and hear her reciting the *23rd Psalm*. This reminded me of happier times and comforted me. After a while, the pain resurfaced again, and I eventually sought a very brief session with a counselor, but I needed more than she offered in order to heal. I sat with my notebook and deconstructed my entire life. Laaawdy!! My pity parties were as grand as a *P-Diddy Party Bus*. You see I was pissed at the Universe and everyone and everything in it.

It finally got to a point where I knew that I needed immediate positive action, or I would implode. So, I prayed for help and soon found myself surrounded by a group of strong, spiritual women who *had wisdom* and with whom I *shared a cultural connection*. These were my earthbound angels who encouraged me to begin to write, breathe and meditate again. Sitting still and clearing my mind calmed me and helped me to think clearly, while writing served to help me put things into perspective and to purge.

They reminded me of my connection with my ancestral mothers and helped me to learn how to use *Ancient African Wisdom Systems* to cope. They also shared their stories with me. The empathy I felt while listening, tapped into my nurturing energy and inspired me to reach outside myself. I immersed myself in community service and created my trademark, KwanzaaMama, Inc. through which I share with children and families the positive aspects of African and African-American history and culture.

KwanzaaMama, Inc. helped me to rise above grief, and with the Creator's help, I learned some practical lessons that helped me to move closer toward healing.

I Learned That I Had to Allow Myself to Mourn

I was beginning a journey that is often frightening, painful, and overwhelming. Someone I loved dearly had died. I was now faced with the difficult, but important need to mourn. My earth-bound angels led me to understand that mourning is the open expression of thoughts and feelings regarding Mom's death. I needed to mourn without shame.

I Learned That My Grief is Unique

Grief is NOT self-pity. It is the process I must go through to be able to accept my loss. If I don't grieve, if I push the pain way down inside, I may seem to be fine on the outside, but inside a time-bomb of emotions is ready to explode or implode. Being afraid of dealing with the pain is normal. However, facing it is necessary. I had to go through the fire and the rain to emerge healed. But I learned that I don't have to do it alone. My Creator is ever present and will send the help I need.

I Learned That No Two People Grieve in Exactly the Same Way

Some people cry and scream while others internalize those feelings, locking them away. A variety of factors that will impact each person's experience include:

1. Their relationship with the person who died.
2. The circumstances surrounding the death.
3. The emotional support system they have in place.
4. Their cultural and religious background.

Because of these factors, grief is unique and personal. Therefore, no one can say how long anyone's period of grief should last. For me, the *"one-day-at-a-time"* approach allowed me to grieve and heal at my own pace.

I Learned that I Needed to Talk About my Grief

At first, I kept the intensity of my grief a secret. But I soon learned that I didn't have to. When I started sharing, I discovered that by expressing my grief openly and sharing my grief outside myself, the process of healing begins. Talking about my grief doesn't mean that I am losing control or going "crazy." It is a normal part of the grieving process. Besides, ignoring my grief won't make it go away. Talking about it helps me feel better. However, I didn't share with just anybody. I opened up to caring people who listened without judging. I sought out those persons who would walk with me on my journey not in front of, nor behind me. At all costs, I avoided people who were critical or who tried to minimize my grief. They would say, "Keep your chin up" or "be strong" or "be happy." While these comments may be well intended, I have a right to express my grief.

I Learned to Expect to Feel a Multitude of Emotions

Losing Mom affected every part of me, especially my head, heart and spirit, which meant I experienced a variety of emotions. I sometimes felt disorganized and heartbroken. I had to allow myself to learn from these feelings and not be surprised if out of nowhere I suddenly experienced surges of grief even at the most unexpected times. Mom and I talked every day. When I got into my car to drive home after work, she kept me company until I was safely home. She was also the one I vented with when angry, and the first to hear my good news. For the first two years after she passed, I would often reach for the phone and had to remind myself that I couldn't call her. This is a natural response to the death of a loved one. I had to give my emotions time to catch up with my reality.

I Learned to Be Tolerant of my Physical and Emotional Limits

Feelings of loss and sadness at times left me feeling tired. Eventually, I had to respect what my body and mind were telling me and take time to:

1. Nurture myself, so I joined a gym.
2. Get daily rest; I went as far as reserving Sundays as my Pamper Day.
3. Eat clean, balanced meals; Ben & Jerry had to stay in the store's freezer.

My earthbound angels reminded me that caring for myself doesn't mean feeling sorry for myself. It means I am using natural survival skills.

I Learned to Develop a Support System
Reaching out to others and accepting support is often difficult for someone as independent as me, particularly when I hurt deeply. I tend to curl into a ball and create distance from others. But I learned that the most compassionate thing I can do for myself during difficult times is to find a support system made up of caring people who will provide the nurturing and understanding I need. They encouraged me to be myself and to acknowledge my feelings, both happy and sad.

I Learned to Make Use of Rituals
A ritual is something done over time in the same way. For example, my morning ritual consists of meditation and reading the magazine "Daily Word," and inspiring books like Iyanla Vanzant's The Value in the Valley and Acts of Faith: Daily Meditations for People of Color. These activities helped me to cope and heal. And I realized that rituals are powerful healing tools, including the funeral ritual, which does more than acknowledge the death of a loved one. It helps provide the support of caring people. Mom's funeral was a way for me to express my grief outside myself. After being designated by the family as the one to write and deliver Mom's eulogy, I realized that if I eliminated this ritual, I'd set myself up to repress feelings and cheat everyone who cares for me of a chance to pay tribute to Mom who was, and always will be loved.

I Learned to Embrace My Spirituality

Allowing myself to be around people who understand and support my spiritual beliefs has been a necessary step toward healing. Some people may believe that "With faith, folks don't need to grieve." Don't believe the hype! I found that I needed to embrace my personal faith, and truly believe that the Creator can fix anything. But, faith without works is dead, so I needed to explore my thoughts and feelings. To deny grief is to invite issues due to the build-up of emotions inside. My motto is, "Keep the faith but express the grief as well." Having the support and guidance of my earthbound angels kept me balanced, but it was my faith in the Creator that brought me through.

I Learned That My Search for Meaning Is Normal

I found myself asking, "Why did she die?" "Why this way?" "Why now?" This search for meaning is another normal part of the healing process. Some questions have answers. Some do not. Actually, the healing occurs in the asking, not necessarily in the answers. My earthbound angels were supportive and listened responsibly during my search for meaning. Besides, I could feel Mom's presence which brought me comfort.

I Learned to Treasure Our Memories

Memories are one of the best legacies that exist after a loved one dies. I was reminded that I should not tuck them away but:

1. Treasure them.
2. Share them with family and friends.
3. Recognize that memories may bring either laughter or tears.

In any case, memories are the important and lasting part of the relationship that I had with a very special person in my life. As I interviewed people in order to include their memories in Mom's eulogy, the joy and laughter shared brought each of us to a place of celebrating Mom for the treasures she left with us.

I Learned to Embrace My Grief and Heal

Accepting that the resolution of my grief would not happen overnight and remembering that grieving is a process helped me to be patient and tolerant with myself. I couldn't heal unless I embraced and expressed my grief. Denying grief only made life more confusing and overwhelming. Embracing my grief helped me to mourn in order to heal and move toward a renewed sense of meaning and purpose in life.

I Learned to Forgive and Let Go

Forgiveness is one of the most important stages of healing grief. I learned that in order to let go of a burden like grief, I had to forgive myself and others. It is not easy because the human mind tends to hold on to stuff especially when loss is experienced. When grief immersed me in the pain of anger, resentment, regret, and blame, my earthbound angels helped me to see that these are all natural, human thoughts and feelings. Most of us have been taught that forgiving is a spiritual act. But I have learned that what allows me to find healing, security and joy is the degree to which I spiritually let go of any thought or feeling that keeps me from forgiving.

The first three years after losing my mother were very difficult for me. Being the spitting image of her, at one point I could not look into the mirror without bursting into tears because Mom and I have the exact same eyes. It took me a while to accept my feelings as normal. And although it was one of the hardest things that I ever had to deal with, I soon realized that as I live life, experiencing the pain of loss and disappointment is inevitable. Still, I can choose whether to and how much to suffer.

One of my biggest breakthroughs was realizing that I had to develop coping mechanisms to deal with Mom's death. I also realized that while the experience may include emotions that we all feel, everyone's encounter with grief is unique. Even though a person doesn't cry, they need the circle of love around them. Like many people, I spoke with I turned inward to cope reflecting on a picture bigger than I had ever considered before.

During this coping stage, my inner self was protected allowing me to continue through the process without requiring permanent changes to my personality. Through this path, I was able to return to a balanced state in which I could once again experience joy. As I lived through the grieving process, I was soon able to relax enough to look at sunrises and sunsets and acknowledge that my Creator had brought me through.

In meditation, I remembered Grandma and Mom leaning on the *Psalms* and the *Book of Job* whenever they were troubled. They taught me that no matter how bad things may look, there is a rainbow after the storm, and although my piece of the world has been altered, I know that I can go through hard times, and like Job come through freshly transformed arriving at the point of feeling alive and engaged again.

To this day, I still hear Mom's voice reciting her favorite Psalm whenever I am troubled. A smile crosses my lips as I reflect on how grateful I am that she, and my elder mothers, taught me the power of Spirit to help me rise above the pain of loss.

In Loving Memory of Mom
Who Taught Me to Believe
Cleo MeriAbut Jarvis
AKA KwanzaaMama

Hope

By Dr. Rochelle S. Jordan

Hope: *(noun): a feeling of expectation and desire for a certain thing to happen. (verb): want something to happen or be the case.*

Throughout my life, I have experienced many trials and tribulations. Some were by circumstance, whereas others were self-inflicted. Today, I live a purposeful life. I have raised a beautiful family, I retired from the military, I am currently on my second career as an advisor for a global Fortune 500 defense contracting firm, and I have completed my doctorate in business administration. Although my early years were bleak and full of uncertainty, I did not let that deter me from living my destiny. One thing that saved me was Hope. I had Hope.

My earliest memories of loneliness, disappointment, and fear were formed in Germany where I grew up. I was six or seven years old and had just completed first grade when one day my mother came home and told my three sisters and me that she was getting married to a man we had never met and that we were moving to Germany. I cannot say how my sisters felt about us being uprooted

111

from everything we knew; our friends, our dad, our grandparents, our cousins, but I looked forward to what I thought would be an adventure.

Growing up overseas was not what I had imagined. My mother was often off to work by the time I woke up in the mornings to get ready for school. In the afternoons when I returned from school, she was already out in the streets drinking at one of her favorite watering holes. Domestic abuse and violence had a strong presence in our five-bedroom apartment in Germany. I often witnessed my mother's husband physically and mentally abuse her. Once, when I was about 10 or 11, my mother swallowed a bunch of pills and climbed out on the roof of our 7th-floor apartment. Horrified, I spent hours convincing my mom to not jump while my stepfather sat idly by. At no point did he try to help her. When she finally came in off the roof, my mother was stoic like a zombie. She remained that way for about three days. This was more like a nightmare than an adventure.

I remember September 10, 1993, the night of my first homecoming dance with my boyfriend, like it was yesterday. We had been anticipating this day for various reasons; it was our parents first time meeting, and we were terrified they could sense I was pregnant. I was a 14-year-old freshman and my boyfriend was a 16-year-old junior in high school. My three older sisters had all become teenage mothers who dropped out of high school and that was looking to be my fate. At first, my boyfriend and I discussed an abortion, but neither of us wanted to ask our parents for help, and because we didn't have any money, that choice was out the window. I knew my mother would be so disappointed when she found out, but there was nothing I could do.

In the summer of 1994, just as I finished up my freshman year in high school, I gave birth to the most beautiful baby girl; 10 fingers, 10 toes, flawless (albeit peeling) skin, jet black, bone straight hair, a cute button nose, perfectly puckered red lips, and almond-shaped gray eyes. I was 14 years old. Shortly after, my family and I moved from Germany back to Louisville, Kentucky, away from my daughter's father and the only life I had known. What was I going to do? I still had a few more years of high school to complete and dropping out was not an option.

My daughter was my motivation. I wanted to give her the best life possible, plus I was determined not to follow in my sisters' footsteps. I wasn't sure how I would navigate the uncertainty of my new life, but I was going to figure it out. Every day was an adventure, and as I settled into my role as a young mother, I began to take a different outlook on life. I fantasized about giving my daughter all the things I had wished for as a young girl, but most importantly I dreamed of stability. Although I didn't know at the time how I would accomplish that, I had hope.

One weekend, my mother dropped me and my daughter off at my oldest sister's house so we could 'catch up,' but several days later when I called to tell her that I was ready to come home, she never showed up. Every week my mother would make an excuse as to why she would not come get me, and eventually I stopped asking. I finally understood what was going on and accepted the harsh reality that my mother had abandoned me when I most needed her. I felt all alone.

Imagine being a teenage mother forced to live in an over-crowded roach-infested apartment in an extremely impoverished community known for crime and drugs. What would you do? I was in a state of shock; my life as I knew it was snatched away and turned upside down. Everything I knew was gone. My new life was extremely mundane. I went to school, came home, did homework, and hung out with my sisters and their friends. There were days when I missed out on the high school social scene; I wanted to run track and try out for the basketball team, but I had other priorities. Some days it was difficult to navigate high school because there were times when I needed my parent's permission to engage in certain school activities or a signature for one thing or another. Given that my mother was no longer involved, I relied heavily on my oldest sister, who is only nine years my senior and at the time had two small children herself, to fill that role.

Things became tense in our household. Food was scarce and there was virtually no money. My sister began asking my mother for the welfare that she was getting for me and my daughter, unbeknownst to me. My mother was extremely selfish and would only allow me to keep the money that I received from welfare, but she would keep half of the food stamps. It was through my sisters' brutal honesty and my mother's actions that I began to see my mother's true self. I grew to despise my mother for making a difficult situation even more stressful to live through. While she lived in a walk-up apartment in a nice neighborhood and never wondered where her next meal would come from, we were starving and forced to figure it out. There were days when I dreamed of living in my mother's home, but I knew those days were long gone; our relationship had changed forever.

At some point during my high school years, I stopped going to class. I would wake up every morning get dressed and then decide that I did not want to make the long trek to school. Because my mother used her address to register me for school, I was assigned to the school in her district. There was no school bus from my sister's house, so I had to catch multiple city buses and then walk about three miles to get to school. I had to begin my journey very early in the morning just to get to school on time. To a kid with a bleak outlook on life, that was a lot to go through to get to a place I did not want to be.

One day, after not having gone to school for about three months, I finally decided that my daughter deserved much better than what I was giving her. I began attending school every day, catching up on all my missed school work, and being the best student I could possibly be. As my high school years came to a close, my guidance counselor, Mr. James Ray took an interest in me. This meant a lot to me since I had never had an adult attempt to guide me through life or tell me that there was life outside of the ghetto.

In my initial meeting with Mr. Ray, I told him about my current living situation and about my strained relationship with my mother. He expressed to me that he had heard 'my story' on more than a few occasions. He felt I was destined for college, but I didn't know anything about college, and I wasn't planning on going. I was struggling to feed my daughter. Where would I get the money to pay for college? Mr. Ray convinced me to have my mother come to the school for a conference so we could discuss my future. In the end, we decided that I would go to college, and Mr. Ray helped me apply for admission and financial aid.

By this time, my relationship with my oldest sister had become so strained, I had to move in with another sister. I had begun working a job and was now completely financially responsible for myself and my daughter; however, I wasn't ready for college. I attended college for about three weeks before I decided it was too demanding for me and I dropped out. The military was my next plan and because I had always dreamed of joining the Army, I walked into the recruiter's office.

I was the perfect candidate for my recruiter; she did not have to convince me to join. I scored well on my entrance exam, we chose my career field, and then it was time to leave. Reality set in that the woman who had abandoned me would have to care for my daughter while I was away in the Army. That was a tough decision to make; still, I knew it was my most ideal opportunity to give her a decent life.

While I was training, I made sure to talk to my daughter every chance I got. I never wanted her to feel abandoned like I had felt so many times or to grow up thinking I chose a life without her. I sent cards and toys and whatever I could think of to keep a connection with her. It was hard being away, but I chose to make that temporary sacrifice.

I met my then husband at my first duty station and we had a whirlwind romance. We were both 19 years old and had only dated for three months before we got married against the advice of everyone who knew us. After settling into our new home, I sent for my daughter to come live with us. Of course, this was not well received by my family, but I thought I knew what was best for her. My husband did not have any children and had never met my daughter nor anyone in my family. In my mind, we were the perfect instant family, but that would quickly come to an end.

The man I married was physically and emotionally abusive. I had ignored all the signs showing me he was controlling, manipulative, and extremely jealous. One particular night, we had been arguing for hours, and I finally went to bed because I had to work the next morning. He came in the room and pulled the covers off me and began berating me. Every so often, he would lunge at me just to see me cower. Then he wanted sex. He kept clawing and grabbing at me and lunging at me so that I'd jump with fear. I was convinced that he would hurt me that night. Although I pleaded with him to stop so I could get some rest, he tormented me for hours until I finally gave up. That was the first time he raped me.

I became pregnant with my second daughter soon after we were married. Adding to the strain of our relationship, he was stationed overseas before our daughter turned a year old and less than two years into our marriage. He returned from his tour a changed man and not for the better. I could no longer withstand his abuse and filed for divorce. It was challenging as a single parent in the military, yet I still had hope that I would be able to provide my girls with the very best life possible. I grew up seeing my mother being physically and mentally abused, and I was going to break that cycle.

Shortly after my divorce, I learned about a program in the Army that would allow me to pursue a college degree. I knew that a degree would expose me to better career opportunities, so I decided to give college another try. The Army afforded me and my girls a secure, financially stable lifestyle, which I had to leave in order to study full-time. I was given a scholarship for college; however,

I had to figure out how to financially support my family. I knew it would all work somehow and could only pray for the best. Through the trials of being a single parent raising two young girls, going to college full-time, and working a part-time job, I graduated college with honors and became a Commissioned Officer in the Army.

There is no magic formula for how I overcame so many adversities in my life. I believe what worked for me was sheer will and determination. Being stubborn helped, too. There were people who wanted to see me fail and I wanted more than anything to prove them wrong. Besides, I was a statistic, and I wanted to escape that stigma. I was never expected to resemble anything remotely close to successful, yet here I am. Fortunately, I also had an awesome support system; friends and family that I could rely on because it truly takes a village.

Throughout the many ups and downs of my life, I have always believed that things would work in my favor. Yes, I worked hard, but making my girls proud was always my biggest motivating factor. If I had not had my daughter, Hope, when I did, who knows where I would be today? It may be cliché, but it is not about where you begin in life, but what you do to change your circumstances. Whatever hand you may have been dealt in life, it is important to remember that we define our own destiny. We cannot let people or our circumstances have power over us. You may feel broken, but you are not defeated. Be encouraged. Hold onto hope and run your race the way you see fit. You are destined to win.

I AM MORE:
Discovering the Power Within
By Monique White, JD, BSN

"There is a 0.8 x 0.7 x 0.9 cm mass which ... contains a cystic component which measures 0.5 cm in greatest diameter."

Have you ever had the rug pulled from underneath you? Been thrown out to sea without a life preserver? Trust and believe, I know what it's like. It can be scary, can't it? Those words above changed my aspirations, my plans, my world.

I just graduated from law school and embarked on my new career. It was the first quarter of my state court clerkship. Visions of a six-figure job, a new home, a new boat, vacations, and financial stability danced before our eyes. It equaled validation. With an unexpected discovery, it all was about to change. I experienced joint pain, swelling, tingling in my hands and feet, and weakness for years. Headaches occurred frequently, but my complaints were brushed aside and dismissed. Doctors gave me a diagnosis of arthritis, fibromyalgia, arthralgias, possible Lyme disease, placed me on medications and sent me on my way.

In the fall of 2002, these symptoms culminated. My mom noticed that I was dragging my leg, and I started stumbling. The annoying tingling in my hands and feet would not go away. My physician at the time took heed and referred me to a local neurosurgeon. Suspicious of MS, the neurosurgeon sent me for an MRI. The results were jarring. I had a lesion within my pituitary gland. As a nurse, I went on high alert. What type of lesion? What did that mean? How was this going to impact my plans?

A pituitary adenoma is a benign tumor. However, they can secrete hormones. In my case, it was a growth hormone. My growth hormone level was off the charts resulting in a condition called acromegaly or gigantism. Acromegaly is a condition where people grow at an excessive rate. Think of Andre the giant or the basketball player Sun Ming Ming. My symptoms were the effects of my body growing after my growth plates were already fused. Subsequently, I met with a world-renowned neurosurgeon to discuss options.

Just prior to my appointment, I had a run-in with a road barrier. I took a turn too closely and scratched up my car. The reason became apparent when the surgeon tested my vision. He discovered a visual field cut. In plain English, I lost a portion of my field of vision due to the tumor. Right then and there, he told me I could no longer drive! I was effectively confined to the house as public transportation was scarce in my town. I was angry. Frustrated. Anxious. Hopeless. Depressed. Isolated. If I couldn't commute to work, how will that affect my clerkship? By extension, how will the impact on my clerkship affect my job opportunities?

Law was my second career. It was a path to a better life. I had it all mapped out. Graduate law school. Finish a clerkship. Land a high paying job. In like manner, I accomplished the first two steps; graduation and clerkship. I was in the process of interviewing for the next step; a firm job. Nowhere in my planning were there steps for neurosurgery and recovery.

So much of my identity was tied to a title. If I wasn't a lawyer, who was I? If I wasn't a registered nurse, who was I? If I wasn't a provider, who was I? I became isolated and depressed. And yes, a little hurt. It hurts when you're alone. It hurts when you cannot support your family. It hurts when you feel unworthy and without value. It hurts.

Growing up, my family placed a lot of emphasis on titles and position. It was a big deal to be a doctor, lawyer, director, etc. It commanded respect. Nothing illustrated this more clearly than my graduation from community college. Not one family member attended. My parents even went on vacation. It's forever stamped in my mind. I asked a lady from church to babysit my son so I could attend graduation. I walked down the aisle and across the stage to receive my degree without fanfare. No one to cheer me on. No one to congratulate me. No one to take pictures. After participating in my friend's photos; I got in the car, drove home, paid the babysitter, and prepared my son and me for bed. Unremarkable.

In stark contrast, my sister's graduation from a four-year college was a big deal. Everyone turned out in full force, immediate and extended family. It was a time of celebration. Similarly, when I obtained my bachelor's degree, they celebrated. My parents, sister, brother, and son cheered as I accepted my diploma. Law school graduation was my parents' joy. My mom wanted everyone there; family, church family, and friends. Through the experience, I learned the value of a title. So, without it, who was I?

With this question in mind, I weighed my options of medical treatment versus surgery. Surgery and recovery would take six weeks. I could do that. I fully planned on returning to work at the end of the six weeks to continue my life plan. In the pre-op area, I remember laughing and joking with my sister. I put on a good face. However, I was apprehensive. I was a single mom. At the end of the day, the buck stops with me. I silently prayed, "God please don't let this man's hands shake." "God if you get me through this, I promise I will slow down. I will take the time to enjoy family and life. I will take the time to smell the flowers." "I promise I won't be so focused on working and making money." Have you ever done that before? Bargain with God? I bargained right up through the backward count into an anesthetic sleep.

After surgery, I woke up miserable. My head hurt A LOT! A baby screamed two stretchers down. There were people talking all around me. Then, the nurse gave me codeine for pain. Codeine is a compound, codeine sulfate. I'm allergic to sulfa. As I immediately started itching and my throat began to close, I thought, "They are trying to kill me." My stay in the hospital and recovery didn't get any better. Upon discharge, I had a splitting headache that would not let up. My head pounded with position changes. My nose constantly dripped. It didn't gush or anything but oozed. Something was wrong.

Time and time again, I returned to the emergency room. I complained to my doctor, neurosurgeon, endocrinologist but no one believe me. No one listened. On one such visit, a surgical resident revealed that the physician's objective was different from mine. My objective was to have the tumor removed. The doctors' goal was not to remove the tumor but to "debulk" it because it was pressing on my optic nerve. In addition to still having the tumor, the resident stated, "You might have a spinal fluid leak. Drink lots of fluid to counteract the effects until it closes on its own."

Of course, drinking lots of fluids did not work. I was so frustrated. I spoke but no one heard. My voice and opinion were devalued. Analogous to a soundproof room, you can beat your fists against the wall, and no one will hear. Finally, the neurosurgeon set up a definitive test. I went for a pledget study. A pledget study involves threading multiple small sponges up your nose into your sinuses then injecting dye into your spinal canal to see if the dye travels to the pledgets. The pledgets remain in place for about 48 hours.

The process didn't go well. An inexperienced first-year resident arrived to inject contrast in my spine. Now, that wasn't going to happen. I demanded a more experienced doctor. Because I refused the first-year resident and demanded a third-year or higher resident (or better yet my neurosurgeon), the radiologist took it upon himself to threaten that I would never be able to have the test done at that hospital. Again, my voice wasn't heard, and my concerns discarded. My voice was devalued.

As you can imagine, my frustration and anger exploded into demands to speak to my neurosurgeon who was away at the time or face a lawsuit. The surgeon apologized profusely when made aware. Magically, a third-year resident appeared to complete the test.

I will never forget receiving the call with results. I was in judge's chambers when the secretary patched it through. The test was positive. Spinal fluid was leaking. My neurosurgeon pleading with me to return to the hospital. He wanted to perform another surgery to fix the leak. Additionally, he recommended I start radiation treatment.

I kindly told him no. I lost trust. He didn't take out the tumor. He ignored my complaints for weeks. He put me at risk for meningeal infection. I needed to find a different surgeon. In the meantime, I bonded with a hired dog walker over our faith. One afternoon, she brought her husband, an OR nurse, over. He asked for permission to take and show my films and lab results to a neurosurgeon at his hospital. Look at God!

Upon review of the data, this surgeon put it this way—have another surgery to correct the problem, or it will eventually kill me. I underwent surgery three months later. It took more than a year to recover. All the while, I watched my classmates move onward and upward. I watched as others graduated and advanced. Little by little, I drew further and further into myself. Frustrated and determined to reclaim some portion of my former self, I made the unilateral decision to go back to work. I wasn't medically cleared. But I refused to feel worthless another day. Accordingly, I began searching for legal employment.

I soon discovered the hard road I had ahead of me. I had this gap in employment. How did I explain it without a) divulging my private health information and b) explain it in such a way that the employer would not assume I had deficits? The legal field is built on intellect and reasoning. Did the surgeries impact my ability to apply logic and reasoning?

A prior experience kept replaying in my mind. In between

surgeries, I attempted to return to work. My boss, exasperated with my focus on work rather than my health, loudly and passionately demanded that I stay home and take care of myself because "you have this thing in your head." I'm sure he didn't mean any harm, but it wasn't the most eloquent way to express his concern and clearly reflected a perception.

Finding a position, any position, proved difficult. I didn't complete my clerkship. I had an unexplained or poorly explained gap in employment. My confidence and self-esteem were low. As rejection after rejection came in, my confidence and self-esteem continued to plummet. It's hard to not take repeated rejection personally. I internalized it. Although friends from law school invited me to social and networking events, I pulled away. The last thing I wanted was to be around people succeeding when I felt like such a failure.

In those times of isolation, it was a struggle to believe that God was there. It was hard to see the purpose. What good was the degree, if I couldn't get a job? What good was a title if I couldn't provide for my family? It took some time, I now see clearly. A situation that could have taken me out didn't. Despite how I felt at the time, I now see God's protection, provision, and purpose throughout.

My experiences shaped me into who I am today. As a result of my experiences, I recognize the power within. I found my voice. I needed to take stock of my internal arsenal and learn how to leverage it. Even though I couldn't see or understand it, it served a purpose. Jeremiah 29:11 tells us, "For I know the plans I have for you, declares the Lord, plans for welfare and not for evil, to give you a future and a hope" (*ESV*).

It was God's plan to teach me:

- My validation comes from above. I was hurt because I sought validation from something and someone other than the Source. My family couldn't do it. My education couldn't do it.

- My worth does not come from the initials behind my name, titles, positions, or material things. It comes from within. My talents, skills, and abilities come from God. It is those talents, skills, and abilities that have a value which manifest in titles, positions, and material things.

- I have the power and authority to change the situation. I am stronger than I once believed. I found my voice in those moments. I have the strength to keep speaking until I am heard. My voice has value.

- God is faithful. Even though I might not see or feel Him, He will never leave me nor forsake me. My hope, trust, and confidence are in Him.

- God has a purpose for my life. There is a purpose in the storm. If it had not been for the storm, I might never have discovered those talents and abilities which saw me through.

- I am a work in progress. Just because I accomplished one goal, doesn't mean I get to stop. Tests and trials will come to refine me. He who began a good work in me will bring it to completion.

My experiences have positioned and qualified me for what I do today. Through them, I discovered who and whose I am, that I am much more than a title, position, or circumstance. Furthermore, my experiences prepared me, so I can lead and minister to women facing similar challenges. I am now qualified to teach others to navigate obstacles, discover, and leverage their unique talents, skills, and abilities to transform their tears to triumph.

"There is a 0.8 x 0.7 x 0.9 cm mass which ... contains a cystic component which measures 0.5 cm in greatest diameter."

Those were the exact words from my MRI. With those words, my world, my plans, my aspirations changed—I discovered my power within. I am more.

Prime Time After 40

By Ingrid Lamour-Thomas

"I know what I'm doing. I have it all planned out—plans to take care of you, not abandon you, plans to give you the future you hope for." ~ Jeremiah 29:11 (MSG)

What if I told you that you have entered the most exciting and rewarding time of your life and you are over 40? What if I told you that you are not behind? What if I told you that it's actually your harvest time? Yes, it is true. Even if you are in the ripe age of *40 something*, you can still have everything you hoped and prayed for in your former years. Indeed, your latter can be greater than your past.

We each have different reasons and different sets of circumstances that have delayed our dreams, callings, careers, businesses, and purposes in life. However, even the perceived delays were ordained by God. Being in Christ, we know that a *delay is not a denial*. And we know that He promises us in Isaiah 55:11, that His word will not return to Him void without accomplishing what He desires. Therefore, living beyond the threshold of the age of 40 can still reveal itself as one of the most exciting and fulfilling times in your life. You can still make an impact. You can still chase your dreams. You can still walk in your purpose and create your own legacy.

First and foremost, my journey started twenty-five years ago when I immigrated from my homeland Haiti to the United States. I remember how nice and warm that afternoon was, like it was yesterday. As a second-year college student, I left my family behind to start a new life thousands of miles away. There was a lot of excitement about me traveling to the U.S. and the day had finally come that I was going to America. An America where, back then, we all had the illusion that it was some far, far away fairy tale country where all your troubles would go away the moment you set foot on this "promised land." Undoubtedly, this was the country of infinite possibilities.

I was traveling to the land where it is possible for all your dreams to come true, a land where opportunities will be knocking at your door the minute you set foot in it. We believed it was the land where all will be well, and life is just going to be good. Granted, it is the place where dreams become reality, but the experience of being here also comes with a lot of work, sacrifices, detours, obstacles, disappointments, humiliations, and many surprises along the way.

Unfortunately, what started as a stage to propel me into my destiny was derailed and seemingly aborted quickly and suddenly. Little did I know that this journey was going to have many detours, ups and downs, highs and lows, mountains and valleys. Next thing I knew, nine short months after I arrived, I was faced with an ultimatum that changed the trajectory of my life in this country. I had to switch gears, put all my hopes and dreams on hold, and focus on survival while fighting my way through and out of many obstacles. From that day, I was on the journey to find my way back to me, to GPS back to the happy, free-spirited girl that I've pushed down and put on the back burner for years.

I finally went back to college in my 30's and graduated with honors. Although I was not a traditional student, I was determined and focused. My undergrad education was all paid for with either grants, scholarships or tuition reimbursement. God made a way and proved that He is and will always be my Jehovah Jireh, the God who provides. I earned my associate and bachelor's degrees in hospitality management and went on to earn my master's in nonprofit management.

Fast forward to being in my 40's and living a life that most people from my country would wish for. From everyone's perspective, I had it all. I was well put together, beautifully dressed and always had a winning smile on my face. All of this after having to go through 20 plus years of struggles, 20 years of pressing through some of the most difficult challenges I've ever had to face in my life, 20 years of fighting for the future I wanted. I had a wonderful marriage and life was good. Still, I was going to a job that didn't give me any fulfillment and I was feeling empty inside. I had to ask myself why was I unhappy? Why was I still unfulfilled? Why is it when I go to work every day my spirit is not overjoyed, and I am so uncomfortable?

I've always been known to be a reliable, hard worker and a great teammate in every job. My job history had been consistent for many years, however, in the span of three years, I have had three different jobs. I couldn't hold a job down. To top it off, my husband who always believed in me, started to lose confidence in me. He said I was the common denominator. That hurt me to my core; it was a tough pill to swallow. But, guess what? The reality is he was right. I was the common denominator. Without a doubt, I wasn't running from those jobs; I was running from my calling.

Even though I looked like I had it all together, something was still missing. I had not become strong enough to chase my dreams. I had not become courageous enough to live my life on purpose and with purpose. That's what concerned my husband. He was frustrated with me not chasing my dreams and not tapping into the gifts and talents God placed on the inside of me. It was time for me to surrender and take a step of faith.

In 2018, the Lord gave me the word *ELEVATE*. He said I'm going to elevate you and expose you this year. He did just that and more. Although I had to take action, He was right there with me to bless and favor me. I took the first step by getting out of my comfort zone and started traveling and going to different conferences all over the country. I started to make connections from each conference which led to collaborations and projects. I've come a long way within the past 12 months, and it is all because I finally said yes to myself and invested in myself.

As a result of me stepping out and taking bold, courageous actions, I became an Amazon bestselling author. I've met my now public speaking coach and started to leverage our connection to fulfill my lifelong dream of being a motivational speaker. In addition, I launched my 501(c)(3) nonprofit organization called Beloved Children and Family Services Foundation serving children and families from low socioeconomic by providing them access to programs, services, resources, education and basic life necessities to lift themselves out of poverty. I also created *The Green Light Movement* which is my empowerment program. All these accomplishments happened in my 40's, all within twelve months. I kept showing up, sowing and pressing on no matter the obstacles, distractions, fear, and hesitation. Despite my fears, I did it all afraid, and now I am reaping the harvest.

Therefore, as we are entering this decade of our lives, whether early, mid or late forties, I want to share with you that this is your *green light season*. God has given you the green light to accomplish the thing that He has placed on the inside of you, to go after your destiny, and to chase your dreams. I encourage you today to reach deep down for the calling that God has placed in you. You have what you need to start. Just begin and let God lead you to the rest.

For the longest, I would tell God things like, I am behind, I should've been further along, my peers are further along in life than me. But He graciously told me, "Daughter you are not behind. It's not too late to use the gifts that I placed inside of you; it's your *"green light season."* You can still chase your dreams with confidence and determination." When I heard those words of blessed assurance, I knew that I had to act swiftly, walk in boldness, and courageously chase my dreams without hesitation.

Time was of the essence, and I am glad I did not delay. Look at the difference God has made in my life in twelve shorts months. And for that, I give Him glory. Wholeheartedly I agree with Dr. Leo Buscaglia who wonderfully stated that *"Your talent is God's gift to you; what you do with it is your gift to God."*

I started **The Green Light Movement** especially to serve and support faith-based professional career women over 40, like me, who appears to have it all together and look successful to the world, but inside there's still a void. They feel like it's too late to chase their dreams, that they are running out of time, or that they have passed their prime time. The truth is I am a living, breathing testimony that we can start afresh after 40. All you need to do is take the first step toward your destiny, your purpose and your dreams. Thus, my desire is to serve women like me who are going to a job every day they hate, but they couldn't leave because they needed the paycheck.

I used jobs as crutches for so long that I became comfortable being uncomfortable. Back then, I was comfortable with the steady paycheck, but I was uncomfortable knowing that there was something bigger in me, that my life was bigger than what I see. Why go to a job and be uncomfortable when God wants you to fulfill your purpose? He is about to resurrect you out of your situations. I pray that God not only uses your gifts and talents, your calling, and your purpose for His glory, but also that He uses your smile, your hugs, your anointing, your encouraging words, your affirmations, and your testimonies. God will surely get ALL the glory and ALL the praise out of your life. Amen? I pray that your whole life reflects how good God is.

Finally, I want to assure you that you are not behind, you have not passed your prime time. You are right on time because you bring wisdom to the table, you bring discernment, experience, maturity, courage, knowledge, patience, compassion and the love of God to the table. We know better and we can do better, so be encouraged and join me on this journey to our next level. You are right on time for this season, for such a time as this. You are ready.

Your audience and your investors are ready to hear from you. You have a voice. They are waiting to hear from you. In fact, they can only hear and receive from you, nobody else.

You are the answer to somebody else's problem and pain. It's not too late to go back to school, it's not too late to start a business, it's not too late to impact a child's life or bring value to someone else's life. It's not too late to be a better person, a better wife, sister, daughter or friend. It's not too late to offer a service or product that your audience is ready and willing to pay for.

Taking the first step and leaving your comfort zone will catapult you to your next level where you will experience the life you hoped and prayed for. However, if you don't start, if you remain stuck and inactive, if you don't activate your calling and destiny, that's when you, my beloved, will run out of time. Therefore, take the leap of faith and use your story and your gift to help somebody else. Remember that *"Each of you should use whatever gift you have received to serve others, as faithful stewards of God's grace in its various forms"* (1 Peter 4:10 NIV).

Again, it's not too late to begin afresh. Here are five ways I stepped out of my comfort zone to pursue my purpose and started to soar after the age of 40:

Work to Create A Mindset Shift

Your mind is a battlefield. Your mindset impacts what you do. We must align our thoughts with the word of God. The way the mind works is the more you tell it something, the more it believes it.

Create Positive Affirmations

Speak life. Remain positive. Your reality will shift as you declare your affirmations. Be aware of what you are saying. Be intentional about silencing toxic words and your own negative self-talk.

Build Meaningful Relationships and Collaborate with Like-Minded Individuals

Take the time to foster these divine relationships. - *"Therefore encourage one another and build one another up, just as you are doing."* - 1 Thessalonians 5:11 (NIV).

Be Consistent

Don't give up. Keep showing up. Keep sowing seeds. Be willing to *"Show up, Speak up, and Follow up."* ~ Cheryl Wood

Be Visible

Your power and your breakthrough depend on you being visible. Come out of the shadows. Your audience is waiting for you. You have a voice. It is powerful, needed and necessary.

It's Not What You Go Through, But How You Go Through It

By Charlease M. Hatchett

God is bigger than any situation on this planet, and I trust Him. Regardless of our situations, I know you and I are meant to live a victorious life, even if it does not look possible in the natural realm. I didn't always think that way, but since I gave my life to Christ at age 9, He has shown me He is a great God. From childhood, I understood that I was covered and well protected. Therefore, whatever comes my way, I can say, "Why not me? "If not me, then who?" As a victor and warrior, I'm here to tell you a cancer diagnosis does not equate to a death sentence. I'm also a survivor who can encourage, educate and equip you with tested applications to navigate the cancer journey. Without a doubt, I believe you too can be victorious as you go through any challenge in your life. I know because, "God is Bigger than Lymphoma©."

In 2014, when I was diagnosed with Non-Hodgkin's Diffuse Large B-Cell Lymphoma, my friends and family had a very emotional response. When I called one friend, she yelled, "Oh no, not you! Oh my God, why did this happen to you? I can't take it; I can't be here without you. You are my sister!" I responded quickly, "Call me when you get it together. I can't handle this right now. Therefore, I waited to tell you; I knew you would lose it," before gently hanging up the phone. My friend literally screamed the entire call, and I was the one with a cancer diagnosis.

My story began with a cough I had for 24 hours straight. When I tell you straight, I mean all day and all night, even in my sleep. Yes, you can cough in your sleep and not really sleep at all. The cough also resulted in me urinating on myself, so I had to take precautions to avoid wetting my clothes. I didn't realize how much I was coughing until my body started hurting. Constantly, I was in pain, sleep deprived and trying to avoid embarrassments when I coughed in public settings.

Initially, I thought it was my allergies, so I went to see my Ear, Nose, and Throat (ENT) doctor who told me I had reflux or GERD. Acid reflux occurs when the sphincter muscle at the lower end of your esophagus relaxes at the wrong time, allowing stomach acid to back up into your esophagus, which can cause heartburn and other signs and symptoms. According to the Mayo Clinic's definition, frequent or constant reflux can lead to gastroesophageal reflux disease (GERD).

I knew I had reflux, but this was somehow different. Although I didn't have heartburn, the other signs were there on and off. It got worse, and I would have a coughing spell for at least 5 minutes straight when I laid down to sleep. It was so bad when I went to the movies; I would apologize before the show began explaining I wasn't sick, I just had a cough. I know that sounds crazy, but it was that persistent.

After multiple visits to the doctor and being diagnosed with an upper respiratory infection, bronchial irritation, asthmatic symptoms, and finally whooping cough, I was exhausted. It was clear the doctors didn't know what the problem was. Thankfully, as a believer, I knew the One who would have an answer, so I prayed and asked God to reveal the root cause of my cough.

I pause here for a moment to give you a warning. Do not ask God for an answer you are not willing to accept. Life happens, and no one is exempt from trials and tribulations. It took me many years to eat and digest this part of my faith walk.

Cancer was my trial and testing of my faith. I know this because I have been told I should not be here. Doctors are often baffled, asking me how did they discover the cancer because it's not often detected early. They were absolutely right. I'm not entirely sure of its cause, although I do have an idea, but that's for another time. Once I began this journey, certain verses had a different meaning to me. This one changed how I viewed my trial as I read, *"And not only this, but we also exult in our tribulations, knowing that tribulation brings about perseverance; and perseverance, proven character; and proven character, hope" (Romans 5:3-4 NAS).*

Now back to my trial relating to cancer and how I woke up to that diagnosis. You see, the coughing was beyond imagination, so my ENT gave me codeine to control it. I didn't understand at the time why it worked, all I knew was it worked, and I was happy. I was down to my last few tablespoons and needed more. Meanwhile, I would take little sips based on my daily activities.

At that time, one of my weekly activities was teaching a Bible study on covenant. As a teacher, I love seeing people's lives change. When the connection is made regarding life issues and they discover them in God's word, it's a light bulb moment. It's a feeling I can't describe, and it makes my heart smile seeing lives restored to God through Christ and His word.

I needed to get through my class without excessive coughing, so I returned to the doctor for more codeine. Keep in mind this was after I prayed for God to reveal the root cause of my cough. At my appointment, the physician's assistant commented on hearing me cough for 45 minutes straight. I replied, "That is why I am here. I'm tired of coughing, and I want answers." She ordered blood work and a chest x-ray. Then I was told to follow it up with a C-T Scan.

Remember, I stated earlier, "Don't ask God for answers you are not willing to accept." Well, I got my answer. Not what I expected, but it was the answer. I was told I had a small mass on my thymus gland, which is located below the collarbone. My options were a biopsy or removal, so I opted for surgery. This resulted in me seeing a cardiothoracic surgeon who would basically crack open my chest to remove the mass. I was excited to have an answer and to know surgery could fix the problem. It was time to stop coughing and urinating on myself and get some long-needed sleep. Before surgery, I knew I needed to pray for the operation to be successful and for a quick recovery. This is where the testing of my faith comes into play.

Unaware that the mass was cancer, I had planned on getting back to my students as soon as I could. I recall encouraging myself to write my prayer for surgery and personalize it, especially covering my surgeon. Not only did I include the surgeon, but also I added the nurses, anesthesiologists, orderlies, housekeepers and others having surgery at the same time. I was told the operation would only take one hour and a half. The doctor was so sure of himself, I could see it on his face. Thank God for prayer and for being His child.

My surgery took 3 ½ hours, and the doctor had to force himself to stop. He wanted to go farther but told my husband he didn't because part of the mass was too close to my vital organs, so he quit. That was only GOD! In my surgical notes, the doctor indicated "It was a very difficult case." You know what he was right? The doctor had told me I would have surgery, go to recovery and wake up in a few hours but that plan did not work. Instead, he had to keep me intubated because cancer tried to infiltrate my left lung.

The tumor was so big; it wrapped itself around vital nerves that controlled lung function. It was so bad on my left side; they had to cut out my phrenic nerve since it was trapped. This was the cause of my coughing all along. The next day after the removal of the ventilator tube, the on-call doctor almost spilled the beans before my husband could tell me what was happening. He quickly took her out of the room before she could finish her sentence. I looked at my son and asked him what was wrong, "Was it cancer?" The look on his face said it all without saying a word. When my husband returned, he calmly told me I had cancer, and that is how I woke up to a diagnosis of Non-Hodgkins Large B Cell Lymphoma.

This is where Romans chapter 5 comes to life. Remembering to whom I belonged lifted me up out of the shock of being told I had cancer. Immediately, I had to take hold of the scripture to encourage and equip myself. Being a sold-out believer in Jesus Christ, serving Him as best as I could to my abilities, did not exempt me from this trial and testing of cancer. But GOD, yes, but God!

My Savior sent the most energetic oncologist to my room to talk with me. I asked, "Dr. Seymour, are you a believer?" and he said, "Yes." He made a statement to me that I didn't understand at the time, but it was a clear form of encouragement and an attempt to lift my spirits. He said, "If you had to have cancer, you have the best type." "What?" I replied, "The best type? How can any cancer be the best one to have?" Another scripture in Romans that I knew applied to me and encouraged me is, *"And we know that God causes all things to work together for good to those who love God, to those who are called according to His purpose"* (Romans 8:28 NAS). This was part of working all things together for my good, so I had to trust in what I knew about my faith and use it on this journey.

Once I was told I had cancer, I did not freak out. I remember telling myself that I am a teacher. I prayed an explicit prayer to God asking Him to keep me here based on kingdom work I had done thus far. This testing of my faith was an opportunity to live out one of my sayings, "It's not what you go through, it's how you go through it." My children have watched me grow in my faith and become a leader in the church and an encourager for others going through issues of life. My son was in college at Baylor University, finishing up exams before Thanksgiving in his junior year. My daughter was 24 years old, working in New York at her first job since graduating Rice University. They were just starting their lives, no spouse, no children, and I wanted to be part of it all.

I had to walk out my salvation in a big way at this point. Without a shadow of a doubt, I knew God was in control; I asked for grace to be extended to me so I could see my family grow and continue to serve Him. As it turns out, God was not finished with me on this earth. I had to go on this journey and be refined in the refiner's fire. I went through a purging process where I had to fight to live.

During my darkest hours, God gave me glimpses of hope, which lifted my spirits and had me encouraging strangers while we were all enduring treatment. He used my network of friends and family to become my intercessors. There were people I didn't plan on telling who prayed for me. I had a plan, but God had another purpose in mind. On one occasion, when my husband was in the middle of deacon training and I was dealing with cancer, I remember going to the bathroom with uncontrollable sobbing. A member who saw me, pulled me to the side and before I knew it, there were three other sisters surrounding me and praying for me. It was a divine appointment. I laugh today because we joke about "Bathroom Ministry." Their husbands were outside waiting on them, not knowing they were covering me in prayer.

As the word got out, the responses were very similar, ones of great shock. Repeatedly, I was asked, "How could God let something like this happen to you?", "You are a teacher of the gospel. Why would God let this happen to you?" Some people were in such shock; some later told me it shook them to their core.

Things were working for my good, and I mostly thank God for praying friends, church family, and my immediate family.

I endured chemotherapy for months, radiation for thirty days straight — three rounds of physical therapy, losing weight and dropping to 134 pounds on a 5'8" frame, blood transfusion and six months later spinal surgery. Yes, that is only the tip of what I have experienced. I am still here today and answering that question my friend had asked, "Oh my God, why did this happen to you?"

Well, as a result of my trial, today I have a personal cancer ministry that I launched, called God Is Bigger Than Ministries©. I also established a cancer ministry at my church called Combat

Ready Cancer Ministry. In addition, I set up a foundation called Connected Through Cancer Foundation. That is how God works all things together for good for those who love Him. He has lifted and launched me so I can lead others based on my cancer journey.

There is so much I would love to share regarding the details of my journey. My goal in life is to educate people about what cancer is and what it is not, how to navigate a cancer journey and come out victorious as a believer. This does not mean everyone will survive, leading to victory on this side. Nevertheless, how we go through this fight against cancer can be a great testimony as we represent the Father before men on this side of glory.

You Can Lift Yourself Out of Past Hurts

By Aida Sanchez

Imagine being daddy's girl and having him snatched from you at the ripe age of nine, due to a homicide. After my dad was murdered, I saw my mom struggle to raise my brother and me, until she met her second husband who respected my mom and provided for our family. Mom was a stay at home mom for more than ten years, however, she became a widow for the second time. I always wanted to know what my childhood beyond nine years old would have been like if my dad had not been taken away from my brother and me at a young age. Not having my dad, was a big loss; I can say I suffered from the father fracture. A little girl needs her father just as much as she needs her mother.

Despite what I didn't have in life, I refused to let it dictate my future. I think back and know that God had downloaded His faith into me before I ever learned what faith was. Faith is the substance of things hoped for, and I truly believed I could have anything I worked hard to get. I loved looking at magazines that caused me to dream and see beyond my environment growing up in the South Bronx. In my area, drugs and gangs were prevalent, as well as fires, which we experienced more than once in the apartment building where we lived.

I have always been called a go-getter from a child and found ways to create multiple streams of income. My ventures gave me a chance to meet others from all walks of life at various networking events and I kept busy. I was content doing what I loved, plus it allowed me to be the best mom I could be to my beloved son. After a few years of being a single mom, I was swept off my feet with irresistible charm.

Even though I carved out time to build on the relationship, I still traveled a lot to build my empire and kept doing what I love as an entrepreneur while working a nine to five. There were a lot of good times as well as times that I would question things and get an excuse. I didn't consider myself being in a domestic violence situation since I wasn't physically being abused, however mental abuse is also considered domestic violence. I'm not one to get so emotional that I lose my self totally and crawl up and die spiritually. However, I questioned myself and frequently wondered how I allowed myself to get into this place. I ignored my inner voice when I prayed and asked God to show me a sign that I should leave, but I never did.

The cheating, lies, and irresponsibility in the relationship were all exhausting. I couldn't understand the behavior as I had never experienced seeing it growing up. I always prayed, but this one time I prayed and asked God to give me revelation knowledge and understanding. Well, you know that God doesn't always answer us how we expect Him to answer. God answered me immediately through a public figure prophet on social media (IG). As I read the post which was titled "Sociopath," and digested the outline, I was shocked and relieved all at the same time. I thanked God for answering my prayer, and I moved on. I don't believe in arguing, fighting or chasing anyone because when we think we're being rejected, we are being redirected to something better for us.

I thank God for equipping me and allowing me to know who I am. I never wore what I was going through at the time on my countenance. It's good I had decided to put God first in my life, which helped me from having emotional meltdowns. Because of my strength, I was always the go-to person. Friends confided in me to talk about what they were going through. I was told that they enjoyed speaking to me since I was nonjudgmental, and I would listen intently.

Whenever someone came to talk to me, I made sure to only say what the Holy Spirit would download in me as I listened. I enjoyed speaking especially with other women because we have been taught to keep things to ourselves and not share negative experiences. However, there are times we all need someone to talk to, whether it's a close family member, friend, or a stranger in the form of counseling sessions. Counseling can be helpful, especially Christian counseling. If you are a believer, counseling can align with God's promises concerning you.

We were created in His image and likeness which means He has given us power and ability to know that we are limitless. He made us to be fearless and to use our brilliance to activate our passions and fulfill our destiny. Winners never quit, we may fall, but we keep getting up and moving forward. Insanity is doing the same thing and expecting a different result. We must dare to be different by doing something different. We must learn to change what we say and think, in order to shift our mindset.

When I decided to launch "Dare to Arise" in Philadelphia with the "It's Your Time to Shine" slogan, it was a prophetic experience. I was driving in downtown Philly, and it was as if God was speaking to me through billboards and paintings on buildings, and signs in stores and restaurants. He made it very clear as I saw signs with the words "mission" and "love" that I was given a mission to go out and impact other women no matter what it looked like. God was also reminding me to walk in love and show love even when I might feel like the other person isn't deserving of it. We will reap what we sow.

I then saw an image with ancient greats and right in the middle was a young woman with long braids that looked like us, which spoke volumes. You must see yourself as great and go out and fulfill your mission as you impact the lives of those assigned to you. Next, there was a mural of people with their arms lifted praising and as a sign of surrendering. I saw another beautifully painted mural with rainbow colors in an abstract form, and they had black metal butterflies attached to the building that reminded me it was my time to help others go through their transformation.

As I drove further down, I saw an old building with an interesting mural in the middle of the building which was created with multi-colored cube like art that had small images in selected cubes, and the word "SHINE" coming down vertically in all white letters. I was just blown away! It was clear I was to have the event when lastly, while at a light, I looked at the street sign on the corner of Rising Sun Ave. There was a Greek Orthodox Cathedral Church on the corner with a man who could have been the pastor standing in the door with one side wide open so that I could see the reflection of the sun shining on the glass of artwork inside. It illuminated like a light.

All these were signs that I needed to see. Also, let them remind you to take heed to the various ways God speaks to us.

Sometimes we can't see the blessing in things, but we must pay close attention. I am glad that I didn't give in to unbelief and decided to move forward with the Dare to Arise Philly event. There were several collaborations that were made at the event with the speakers, an attendee and me. Opportunities were birthed out of the event and I was excited with the outcome. The owner of the Execute That! Studio who is a pastor also gave me a prophetic word. I had a chance to see a young man share a dream that I told him would come to pass and it did a few months later in Hollywood. He is now on his journey along with his mom making a mark in this world that can never be erased.

Since I am still employed full time, I have accepted the fact that it's okay to do things at my pace. We must walk by faith and not by sight. When we believe that we can do anything we set our minds to accomplish, we will do it. The key thing is always to live by faith and surround yourself with like-minded people. We can't move forward surrounded by naysayers and those that are complacent. We should focus on destroying generational cycles and encourage one another to live out our passions and to live out loud to impact the lives of others.

With over 30 years of experience in various fields of business and public speaking, I have decided to get coached in order to lead other women, and encourage them that they too can LIFT, LAUNCH, LEAD. I have always enjoyed coaching other women; however, I have been taught to monetize my skill sets and not feel guilty about it. Everything I teach is duplicable, so the results can be seen repeatedly. I have written a chapter in several anthologies and will team up with a group of women that would like to join me in this venture soon.

I am building a course to teach on how we can A.R.I.S.E. (Activate-Rich-Identity-Successful Empire). Everyone has the same opportunities presented to them. We must make a wise decision to say YES to ourselves so that we can arise and shine for the world to see. We tend to talk to some people repeatedly, but instead, we should work to lead them as that's the greatest way to impact an individual's lives.

I had to decide to move past my circumstances by shifting my mindset. It has been proven that our thoughts dictate our feeling and our feelings dictate our actions and our actions dictate our results. I also know that what we make happen for others, God can make happen for us. I decided to lead where I am and not wait for things to appear perfectly or the right time. As we know, there will never be a perfect time.

As we share our stories, it allows us to heal and level up in our work. I believe that authenticity and transparency is key in helping others. Everyone doesn't look like what they have been through. We learn about what others have overcome as they share their story, so we in turn should free ourselves and do the same. We are not our past, but our past prepares us for where we are heading in our individual lives. We all have our individual paths to travel, but we all have one thing in common, which is to impact the lives of others in order to help them to lift themselves out of their circumstances.

I encourage you to lift, launch, and lead now. You have everything you need to move forward and live the life you dreamed of. Nothing happens unless you decide to take action to activate your vision. Take time to write the vision and work daily on the goals that will change the trajectory of your life and the lives that you will impact. Don't wait another day, choose today to make the change and invest in you, you are worth it. It all starts with a mindset shift and knowing that we are more than enough.

We have everything that we need in us to do what all we need to do. We can live a fruitful life even after a major break up. We are worthy and more than enough, and don't have to stay in unhealthy relationships, for fear of being alone. It's essential to feel good about ourselves in whatever state we find ourselves in at any given time. All the trials are to make us stronger, and we can take the pain and turn it into our passion.

However, are you feeling stuck, unfulfilled, uninspired, or just feeling like you have reached a plateau on your current job? Do you feel uncertain of how to change careers and pursue your dreams? If that's you, let's shift lanes and make the connection that will help activate the vision. Let's stop wasting precious time, that can never be gained back, and let's redeem the time we have left to ARISE and Shine. The world is waiting on you; your story matters. You don't have to do this alone, and I look forward to speaking with you to discover how I can help you shift gears and move forward with your vision. To connect with me, you can choose from the following: AidaLSanchez.com, Instagram @AidaLSanchez and Facebook Aidal.sanchez also Aida Sanchez.

Conclusion

By Donna Hicks Izzard

G iven the fact that life is not always a bed of roses, we are all bound to encounter challenges at one point or the other. Unfortunately, the pain of these trials can cause women to feel inconsolable and that they don't have a stress absorber. Considering this, we focused on the realities of life with emphasis on the ups and downs.

This book reveals that regardless of how smooth sailing everything appears, there may come a time when life just doesn't seem to be going your way. Perhaps you have had similar experiences, or there was a seasonal flow when you felt like nothing was functioning and everything was out of whack, and you found yourself questioning, "why me"?

The chapters in LIFT, Launch and Lead demonstrate a wide-range of experiences the co-authors guide you through. These chapters reveal that regardless of the different twists and turns you take in life, your current situation can and will change if you have faith and trust in God. To this end, many of our co-authors have shared their true-life stories in this resourceful anthology to renew hope as well as resuscitate the will of other women whom might have given up due to the challenges they faced with similar experiences.

More instructively, each chapter of this book illustrates powerful messages that you should always trust and commit to your faith. Some chapters share that if you trust God and fervently adhere to HIS word, you will find yourself on a journey toward the fulfillment of your desires, dreams, and destiny. Other chapters state that what is most required of you is to humble yourself with the intent of being capable of launching yourself to another position upon which you can then fulfill your purpose. Additionally, each author presents various storms that communicate different experiences that are capable of discouraging you from launching and fulfilling your purpose throughout the plot of the book. It was therefore vividly clear, there is no doubting the fact that faith plays a huge role for many of the authors. This is justifiable by the actions that they have outlined in the book, where they relied on their faith to sail through daunting challenges.

Drawing from the ladies' heartfelt testimonies, there is an obvious impression that you can lift yourself out of any situation and you'll be able to lead others to launch their own testimonies. This is a practical book that will demonstrate that your dreams will not die if you stay faithful and committed to them regardless of any circumstance. Above all, our message is that if you learn to trust God and believe that you can do all things through Christ who strengthens you, it will position you on a plan to LIFT, LAUNCH and LEAD towards your destiny.

ABOUT THE AUTHORS

Dr. Ranelli Williams

Dr. Ranelli Williams is a best-selling author, speaker, workshop leader, entrepreneur, and Certified Public Accountant and co-owner with her husband, Eric of ERJ Services, a boutique tax and accounting business. They help their clients keep their business financial data organized efficiently, pay only the minimum legal taxes, and maximize their profits.

She is also The Legacy Catalyst, empowering faith-based entrepreneurs and couples to give their children a head start by leaving them a legacy of faith, of business ownership, of money mastery, and of generational wealth-building.

Dr. Ranelli is also co-founder of the LIFT Conference, a faith-based conference that has served hundreds of women in business and ministry. Her motto is "Let's build those legacies and be the last generation that has to start over without a strong financial foundation."

Contact:
Website: www.ranelliwilliams.com

Donna Hicks Izzard

Author, Speaker and Master Business and Branding Strategist Donna Hicks Izzard is an exceptionally gifted woman with vision. As intuitive as she is inspirational, she helps highly successful corporate professionals to blend their expertise and brilliance into profitable, passion-fueled businesses while maintaining their full-time careers. Under Donna's tutelage and enlightening insight, her clients become more than entrepreneurs with side hustles—they become CEOpreneurs with empires.

Revered for her ability to build a brand, Donna is masterful at devising innovative strategies to elevate people to their next level. Be it in a coaching session or a simple conversation, she is an ignitor—of souls and ideas—setting people on fire to go out into the world and pursue their purpose.

Donna currently resides in New Jersey with her family, but she is devoted to empowering young women and single mothers in Harlem, New York where she was born and raised.

Contact:
Website: www.donnaizzard.com

Kim Jones

Motivational speaker, certified personal life coach, bestselling author and playwright, Kim Jones has an extensive background in the area of corporate training, empowerment coaching and career development. Using her extraordinary gifts and working in the capacity of a speaker, trainer, and coach has evolved her into a skilled facilitator with the ability to connect with and inspire any audience.

Kim enriches audiences with her earthy, savvy, and charismatic appeal. She also uses her talents and skills to write creatively and express life through plays. Her love for writing is now coming to life through stage plays and short stories, like "Sis. Ruby's House."

Kim's relationship with God has allowed her to step out on faith and bring to life her vision of writing and producing. She looks forward to being on the big screen and making motion pictures.

Contact:
Website: www.iamkimjones.com

Donna Heath-Gonzalez

Donna Heath-Gonzalez is President and CEO of Big Apple Beauty Supply, Inc., BABSHair.com, and LadyD's Hats & Fascinators. In 2004, Donna obtained her BBA in Accounting from Baruch College; first in her family. She is a mother, grandmother and an avid supporter of her community. Donna supports several women's organizations and has sponsored the Mrs. NJ/PA United States Pageant in 2017 and 2018 where she was honored with the Civil Leader Award.

Donna has provided her community with several "give-back initiatives" such as: Thanksgiving turkeys; back-to-school supplies, prom dresses and dinner with gifts for the elderly. In addition, she established the Big Apple Beauty Supply Scholarship in August 2018 and does this through her non-profit organization.

Donna was awarded the 2018 Business Woman of the Year Award by BW NICE Monroe County Chapter at their Red Shoe Luncheon for charitable work in her community.

Contact:
Email: donna@bigapplebeautysupply.com

Chaundra Nicole Gore, MSL

Chaundra N. Gore, founder and CEO of Lens of Faith Photography, LLC and LensOfFaith Speaks, is a motivational speaker, author, leadership strategist and a master sergeant in the U.S. Army. She hosts her own podcast, Thursday Night at 8 w/ LensOfFaith.

Chaundra is a member of Kappa Epsilon Psi Military Sorority Incorporated, Brand Ambassador for We Are Women of Substance, Brand Ambassador for L.I.F.T (Ladies Intentionally Following Through), and Brand Ambassador for Black Women Handling Business. She is a survivor of domestic violence and sexual abuse and is an advocate for victims of such abuse.

Chaundra and her beloved husband Kenneth D. Gore Jr. has a blended family of seven children. She is from Chicago, IL and recently settled in Lithia, FL.

Chaundra has a Bachelor of Science in Business Management, a Master of Science in Leadership and is currently pursuing her doctorate at Grand Canyon University.

Melissa Castro-Wilson

Melissa Castro is a coach, speaker and author. She is the founder and CEO of Latinas Launch, an organization that provides coaching services to equip and empower women to walk in their God-given purpose and chase after their dreams. It is her desire to foster a community where women can grow spiritually, physically, mentally and financially.

Ms. Castro graduated from Lehman College with a Bachelor of Arts in Latin American Studies. Along with operating Latinas Launch, she currently works full-time in Real Estate Property Management in New York City.

Melissa was born and raised in The Bronx, NYC and continues to live there today. She is the mother of two amazing children, Destiny (21) and Elijah (17).

Contact:
Facebook: coachmelissacastro
Instagram: @coachmelissacastro

Khalima Green

Khalima Green is the CEO of Lady Kay Enterprise, an empowerment speaker, transitional divorce coach, author, and community advocate. She spends her days helping women navigate their way through the personal and emotional side of divorce, becoming a single parent and starting over.

Khalima's divorce experience drove her to become more responsible and literate on the subject. She intends to use her business management and finance education from East Stroudsburg University to teach similar women about wealth and financial literacy. With over ten years of diverse experiences in business, her goal is to assist them in taking control of their lives and reclaiming their independence.

In her spare time, Khalima prefers to spend time with family and travel. She resides in Pennsylvania where she chairs the health committee for the NAACP Monroe Chapter and sings on the praise team at Mountaintop Church.

Contact:
Email: info@ladykaycoaching.com

Cheray Diggs

Cheray E. Diggs loves to work with people. She is a healthcare professional with over 25 years of experience as a Medicare Analyst. Cheray is a certified medical assistant and is working on her certification in medical coding and billing. Currently, as a medical assistant, Ms. Diggs enriches the lives of others and teaches them how to navigate in this field.

Cheray is no stranger to community relations. Her passion is to serve. She worked alongside her beloved grandmother who was a community advocate. Cheray also volunteered at The East Harlem Tutorial program and at food pantries in the Bronx and Harlem communities.

Cheray's Christian faith has led her to Agape Impact Ministries under the teaching of Pastor E. Derrik Porter in Harlem, New York. She gives God all the glory.

Contact:
Email: Cheray2061@gmail.com
You can also find her on FB and IG.

Vanessa I. Farrell

Vanessa I. Farrell is the CEO and founder of Vanessa Ingrid Health & Wellness Coaching, LLC.

As a certified health coach, Vanessa is passionate about healthy eating and active living. She serves as an ally who helps women and girls gain the necessary knowledge and skills to be active participants in achieving their health goals. Ms. Farrell is excited to celebrate her clients as they become empowered ambassadors of their well-being.

Vanessa earned her undergraduate degree in health and nutrition sciences and her graduate degree in public health (MPH) from Brooklyn College. She received a certificate in health coaching from the University of North Carolina Greensboro and is a Master Certified Health Education Specialist (MCHES). This anthology publication is her first, launching her into the author sphere.

Vanessa was born on the beautiful island of Montserrat and currently resides on the island of St. Croix in the United States Virgin Islands.

Diann Antley

Diann Antley is the president and CEO of Anew You Travel, LLC, a full-service travel agency that has won the Pocono Record 2018 Readers' Choice Award for Best Travel Agency. As a travel consultant, she helps numerous professionals take vacations they desire and deserve to regain passion in their lives.

Diann knows what it is like firsthand to go from broke and broken to repaired and renewed. Her experiences motivate her to help other women to be restored. Whether it's from assisting with a great vacation, telling her story to uplift others, or coaching them on ways to transform their lives, Ms. Antley is dedicated to inspiring women who cross her path.

Besides being a successful entrepreneur, Diann serves as an executive member of the Monroe County Chapter's NAACP, is a member of various networking groups, and participates in several ministries at her church.

Contact:
Email: diannantley@gmail.com
Phone: 570-236-8340

Rev. T'Shawn Rivers

T'Shawn Rivers is a seasoned business professional with over twenty-five years of experience in senior management, fundraising and technology. She began her career as an associate director of Finance and Administration at the American Museum of Natural History in New York and progressively increased in status to the position of Director of Institutional Advancement. Ms. Rivers' notable achievement made her the first African-American to become a director of development within a renowned non-profit.

T'Shawn is a published author and is in the process of starting a consulting business. She is a proud participant of the LIFT Conferences in the Pocono Mountains of Pennsylvania and has served as a LIFT Conference Ambassador in the Fall of 2017 and 2018.

T'Shawn currently works as a senior director of Development and Partnerships at Race Forward in New York. She is married with two adult children and is a devoted grandmother of three granddaughters.

N. Lynne Henderson

Entrepreneur, e-commerce strategist, author, speaker, and trained culinarian, Lynne Henderson has a passion for encouraging and empowering others to become entrepreneurs. Prior to her self-employment journey, Lynne was employed in the financial, non-profit, and education sectors.

Ms. Henderson recently launched The Partea Chef Baking & Culinary Classroom, a virtual community that teaches new bakers/cooks to increase their culinary skills by building a solid foundation that will enable them to start a culinary business if desired. As an e-commerce strategist, Lynne helps individuals pursue financial independence by training them to create additional streams of income via e-commerce platforms.

Lynne's faith plays a major role in her life's endeavors. She serves in the local church as a licensed minister and worship leader. Her favorite quote is "when life gives you lemons – make lemonade."

Contact:
Email: Gracelynnellc@gmail.com
Facebook: N. Lynne Henderson Instagram: @Grace_lynnie

Rosie Thames

Rosie Thames is a devoted wife and mother of three phenomenal children. She is an active duty Air Force member, servant-leader, mentor, speaker, successful entrepreneur and an overcomer. Hailing from Kingston, Jamaica, Rosie's vision is to empower others to succeed despite adversities and inspire people to leave a legacy for generations to come.

In 2015, Rosie and her husband became top income earners in their company. They launched Growing to Greatness, LLC and Team No Limit, teaching people how to leverage the direct sales industry and earn significant income from home, become debt free, and live life on their own terms. She coaches entrepreneurs by using the strategies and methods she used to grow her own business and develop her as a leader.

Rosie's passion is to impact lives, bring hope, healing and transformation by supporting and motivating others to live their best life and dream big.

Darice Mechelle Stephenson

Founder and CEO of Lifestyle Wellness Group, LLC., Darice Stephenson's passion is to help others fully gain and successfully maintain their own health and wellness goals.

For over 15 years, Ms. Stephenson has utilized a collaborative approach to personally explore the specific health concerns of her clients as they discover the tools necessary for a lifetime of nutritional balance. As a Certified Health Practitioner with the American Association of Drugless Practitioners, Darice uses holistic, interactive methods to help clients navigate through inconsistent nutritional advice to determine what is necessary for their optimal care.

Darice holds two degrees, an MHA and an MBA, plus she is highly trained as a Health Coach through the Institute of Intergraded Nutrition (IIN) in New York City. She leads workshops and interactive healthy cooking classes as a Certified Raw Food Chef. Working with other industry experts, she is continuously impacting the world to be healthier.

Cleo MariAbut Jarvis

Cleo MeriAbut Jarvis is an award-winning educator, poet, story-teller as well as a recognized resource for implementing service projects in schools. She utilizes her trademark KwanzaaMama, Inc. to provide education and service to others. As KwanzaaMama, Cleo spearheads the *Kwanzaa Community Celebration* FREE to the community, and the JuneTeenth Freedom Festival.

Heralded for her leadership in molding children as young as seven years old into philanthropists and community service advocates, Cleo has earned prestigious service awards, including The Jefferson Award for Public Service, the Excellence in Service Award from NYC Department of Education and the Mayor's NYC Service Award. She is also a prolific writer who has published several titles and was a co-author in the LIFT Next Level Anthology.

Ms. Jarvis is passionate about bringing cultures and communities together, and shares insights into her ongoing projects and workshops on her website.

Contact:
Website: www.KwanzaaMama.com

Dr. Rochelle S. Jordan

Dr. Rochelle S. Jordan was born in Louisville, Kentucky. She is a self-proclaimed military brat who grew up in Schweinfurt, Germany. Dr. Jordan is a proud decorated combat veteran, having deployed to both Iraq and Afghanistan.

Rochelle's educational achievements include receiving a bachelor's in psychology, a dual master's in information technology management and management and leadership, and a doctorate in business administration with a focus in leadership. She is committed to help others realize their educational goals and loves to advise young people of possible career choices.

After retiring from the United States Army, Dr. Jordon settled down in Texas where she serves as an advisor for a global Fortune 500 defense contracting firm. She's the proud mother of three and Nana to the sweetest toddler. In her spare time, Rochelle can be found reading and traveling all over the world.

Contact:
Email: rochelleshivon@yahoo.com.

Monique White, JD, BSN

Monique White is an attorney, registered nurse, certified life coach, and speaker. She is the founder of Triumph Services, LLC where she provides coaching and consulting services to break chains and transform lives. Ms. White strongly advocates for the disadvantaged through her combined expertise in law and nursing.

Evident throughout her career, Monique has a servant's heart. Her transparency of her own life experiences inspires women to discover and leverage their abilities to transform frustration into motivation and anxiety into abundance. Her core belief is as God's daughters, we are more than circumstances or situations.

Ms. White has earned an Associate Degree of Nursing, a Bachelor of Science in Nursing, and holds a Juris Doctor degree from Rutgers School of Law. She also has a certificate in professional coaching from Community College of Philadelphia and multiple national nursing certifications in her specialties.

Contact:
Website: www.triumphsvcs.com
Facebook: triumphsvcs Instagram: @triumphscoach

Ingrid Lamour-Thomas

Ingrid Lamour-Thomas is a motivational speaker, author and the founder of The Green Light Movement, LLC. She is also the founder and CEO of Beloved Children and Family Services Foundation, Inc., a 501(c)(3) nonprofit organization, which has been nominated for two prestigious awards, serving both her homeland, Haiti and her community in Orlando, FL. Its mission is to provide services, education, nutrition, and basic life necessities to children and families from low socio-economic communities.

Ingrid has a master's degree in Nonprofit Management. Her personal mission is to empower, impact, and bring value to someone else's life by providing support, encouragement and hope through service. She is passionate about motivating women to believe in themselves and in their abilities and to walk in confidence. Ingrid is a servant leader and she wants to see women win. That's her heart's desire.

Contact:
Email: www.thegreenlightmovement.com

Charlease M. Hatchett

Charlease Hatchett is an international bible study teacher and cancer survivor. For over 20 years, she has been engaged in bringing people closer to the word of God as well as devoting her time to volunteering for various causes. She is a former volunteer with Precept Ministries as well as an international women's retreat coordinator.

More recently, Charlease became an entrepreneur. She is the founder and CEO of God is Bigger Than Ministries. Additionally, in the cancer space, as a survivor, she wanted to equip and support those going through their healing journey, so she created the Combat Ready Cancer Ministry Program at Fallbrook Church in Houston, TX. She's also the founder and CEO of Connected Through Cancer Foundation, a 501(c)(3) organization.

Charlease received her B.S. degree from Longwood University in Virginia. She currently resides in Spring, TX with her husband J. Harold Hatchett, III and has two adult children.

Contact:
Website: www.godisbiggerthanministries.com
Email: ctcf@gmail.com

Aida Sanchez

Aida L. Sanchez is a speaker, author, coach, visionary and entrepreneur. Her passion is to see other women live a transparent, authentic, bold and fearless life. She works with clients who are ready to activate their rich identity and build a successful empire. Ms. Sanchez encourages them to GLOW UP together.

After many years of investing in conferences, coaching, empowerment and entrepreneurial events, Aida decided to launch her business and build her million-dollar brand while she continues to work her 9 to 5 as a HR professional. She has coached others who have started their successful business while working a 9 to 5. Aida believes in generational wealth building in order to leave a legacy for your children's children.

For upcoming conferences, webinars, workshops, ARISE course, and future book, you can connect with Aida via her website where you can also sign up for your free discovery session.

Contact:
Website: AidaLSanchez.com

CPSIA information can be obtained
at www.ICGtesting.com
Printed in the USA
FSHW011521310519
58508FS